THE HUMAN SIDE OF POLITICS

Douglas Roche, M.P.

THE
HUMAN
SIDE
OF POLITICS

CLARKE, IRWIN & COMPANY LIMITED
TORONTO / VANCOUVER

Canadian Cataloguing in Publication Data

Roche, Douglas J., 1929–
  The human side of politics

ISBN 0-7720-1089-7

1. Roche, Douglas J., 1929–   2. Canada – Politics
and government – 1963– *   I. Title.

FC626.R62A34   971.06'44'0924   C76-017144-0
F1034.3.R62A34

ISBN 0-7720-1089-7

Published simultaneously in the United States
by Books Canada Inc., 33 East Tupper Street,
Buffalo, N.Y. 14203

and in the United Kingdom by Books Canada Limited,
17 Cockspur Street, Suite 600,
London SW1Y 5BP.

1 2 3 4 5 6   JD   81 80 79 78 77 76

Printed in Canada

For Eva

and

Evita, Mickey, Doug, Mary Anne and Patti

ACKNOWLEDGEMENTS

Authors know how lonely is the creation of a book. Support comes from many sources, often in unexpected ways. My family, first of all, has helped me more than they know. I am grateful to several parliamentary colleagues who have provided valuable insights into their own feelings about this frenetic existence. The Parliamentary Librarian Erik Spicer and the chief of Parliamentary Research Philip Laundy have extended professional courtesies to me without stint, as has Robert Miller, research officer in the Parliamentary Library.

Two men, John Thompson and Ralph Gorman, C.P. who were my editors in earlier years, deeply influenced my thinking. Harold Alston's friendship was but one blossom of the ecumenical movement. I cannot name here all my Edmonton friends who have helped me in my political life but they know the strength they have given me.

Two author-friends Gary MacEoin and John Patrick Gillese gave me valuable help in writing this book by criticizing a first draft. Ruth Fraser, my literary agent, gave me the confidence I needed to pursue the book to completion. I thank, finally, my secretaries Pamela Miles and Betty Mitchell, who along with Ann McCorquodale, Janet Belyea, Anne Warren, Mollie Doyle, Jean Cochrane, Olive Howlett, and Margaret Law worked so diligently on the preparation of the manuscript.

Ottawa, July 1, 1976

CONTENTS

INTRODUCTION

OF ASTRONAUTS AND MEMOIRS

I remember when I turned forty (just a few years ago), telling people that it was a difficult age—too old to be an astronaut, too young to write my memoirs. Whatever changes of life occur as a man comes into his fifth decade, mine included a plunge into federal politics. I discovered, vicariously indeed, that politicians do have something in common with astronauts: an eerie feeling of weightlessness, a removal from the familiar reality, a sense of disorientation. At the same time there is the overpowering feeling that we are going somewhere, even if the destination is uncharted. There's action all around us, though we ourselves may be doing nothing. I shouldn't push the similarities too far, however. Astronauts know when they have achieved their goal and so does everyone else. Not so politicians— unless you count winning elections as a demonstrable goal. Which I don't.

And that brings me to the subject of memoirs. After twenty or thirty years in the business politicians sometimes write their memoirs. The books often turn out to be reflections, properly matured, on historical events; an edited version of old speeches, or famous-people-I-have-known, usually with a little spice. All of these approaches have their own merits.

As of this moment I have been a Conservative Member of Parliament for three years and eight months. Not long enough to have acquired more wisdom, if any, than I brought to the job. (Not long ago, I saw a sign outside a church near Parliament Hill: "If the world could be saved with wisdom, it would have been saved a long time ago.") Neither have I made enough speeches nor collected enough tidbits to hold a book together. I did shake hands with Premier Kosygin of Russia, but he looked right through me; and my chance to meet the Queen was thwarted by political conniving that dispatched dinner invitations only to Liberals. I stood in a semi-circle with Indira Ghandi of India at a reception—hardly material for an epic.

What I have developed is a sense of outrage at the parliamentary process. My feelings are deep and I think it would be a mistake to wait until the end of my career to express them. For I believe that mankind has entered a new stage of civilization. We are now a world community with dynamic technological, cultural and social change all around us. The magnitude of this change is comparable to the change from an agricultural to an industrial society. Questions of life and death on a global level are now in our hands.

I am not a doomsday merchant, but we do not have a generation or so to contemplate present problems in the unspoken hope that they will go away. Our political process is scandalously deficient in resolving problems and creating a society of peace and social justice. As one who participates daily in the mysterious world of politics, I have experienced enough to issue this plea for a new direction *now* in politics and society. We have got to stop passing on the really big problems to the next generation while we apply bandaids to the open sores. That is how we have been conducting affairs for a very long time.

The problem of a new direction is not only conceptual, it is political. For the political systems of all societies reward leaders for maximizing present benefits to the people while passing on the costs to other countries and future generations. The interlocking nature of modern global problems—mass poverty, food shortages, energy depletion, the arms race, monetary breakdowns—should suggest to us that it is in our enlightened self-interest as Canadians to work for their solution.

As far as I am concerned the place to concentrate a reformist approach is in Parliament. Political power is by no means confined to Parliament Hill; it is all around us—in big business, unions and international protest movements. But Parliament is the central forum of our country. It sets the tone of public life and its decisions are felt by every Canadian.

The theory behind Parliament is wonderful. But given its present operation and the urgency of meeting the demands of this new era, it has to be said that politics in Canada is a shallow game. Examined closely, its results are shabby—and short-sighted. Politicians and the public are both culpable, but the full basis of our ineffectual political system is found within our way of life.

Parliament is replete with posturing windbags who think power is an end in itself. Statesmanship is measured in unconditional government grants. The electoral process is dominated by political organizers who manipulate the public through the adroit use of television. Politicians in all parties continue to behave largely as though we stand upon solid foundations which need no examination. The public seems to be indifferent.

Fundamental questions about the kind of world economic system and social order we wish to have are staring us in the face. But they have little priority in our discussions and elections. When a group of nationally known religious leaders complained during the 1974 federal election that vital issues of global social justice were being ignored, the churchmen themselves were ignored. At several all-candidate forums I raised the issue of Canada's role in an interdependent world and received very little response. The audiences repeatedly drove me back to my stand on domestic inflation and capital punishment.

But I'm getting into the substance of this book. I merely wanted to state here why a practising politician is writing a book that is neither memoirs nor inside revelations of party politics. The fact is, all political parties and governments are confronted by the same problem, namely, how to hold society together in the age of "future shock."

There are crucial moral questions at the heart of the human dilemma today—the growth ethic, the right to life, social justice at home and abroad—and it is these topics that I address in this book. I reject any reaction that I am merely presenting idealism when the real work of Parliament is to run the country on a day-to-day basis. Our failure as a society—our failure in Parliament—in setting human goals and preserving values in attaining them has brought on a sense of disillusionment in modern society. We don't need any more parliamentary tinkering under the guise of realism. What we need is a chart—in broad social, economic and political terms—to show where we are going as a people. I want Parliament to be actively engaged in the examination and articulation of social values, sensitive to the quality as well as the quantity of Canadian life. That, to me, is the most realistic kind of politics. And also the most human.

THE HUMAN SIDE OF POLITICS

{1}

FROM SANDY HILL TO PARLIAMENT HILL

Often when I am sitting in the House of Commons in the midst of the fights, posturing and droning on that take up so much of the parliamentary day, I think of three men far from Parliament Hill who, in the chance encounters of life, were largely responsible for my decision to become an M.P. Krishnankutty of India. Aristides Bastidas of Venezuela. James Ibole of Nigeria. Those three men, from such different backgrounds, helped me to understand what the phrase "global village" means. I met them during my travels as a journalist in the 1960s. Our lives touched for only a few days but this was long enough to open my eyes to the reality of the human condition today.

⌘

A westerner can hardly walk unobtrusively into a village in India, but even so I wasn't prepared for the sensation I caused when I sought out a farmer named Krishnankutty. A hundred farmers gathered around me as I set out across a field of sugar cane which glowed with a mauve reflection of the setting sun.

Krishnankutty showed me his clay hut with a straw roof which he had built himself. He was glad, he said, that it didn't leak very much during the monsoons. The only furniture in the three small, dark rooms were a few benches and some straw mats spread on the floor for sleeping.

His six children, aged seventeen to two, joined the cluster around us. I could see their scabies and eczema and the strange shape of

1

the bodies of the little ones caused by a diet severely low in nutrition. Krishnankutty's wife Karthiayini, who looked much older than her thirty-five years, told me that the children get tapioca with a little rice twice a day. "Sometimes when we have the money, we give them a little breakfast of coffee or tea," she said. The children never get milk.

By his own standards Krishnankutty is a simple man who wants a better home and education for his children and a regular income. These simple desires have been a powderkeg in Kerala, a small southern state that has been a centre of interest in India. Although Kerala is a stronghold of Christianity in India, it was the first place in the world ever to adopt a Communist government in a free election.

Kerala is described by the travel books as a palm-fringed paradise. There is no denying the appealing groves of tropical fruit and the carpet of brilliant green in the rice paddies. But a more realistic view of the lives of Krishnankutty and his fellow villagers was uttered by a missionary: "They work, they starve, they love."

The world for Krishnankutty is some far-off place. He only hopes that in his next incarnation he'll be born into a higher caste and have a better share of life's goods. Once in a while he walks a mile to the house of his friend Philip Paulose, a doctor, and listens to the news on the radio but he finds everything far beyond him. Every two or three months he finds a little release from his cares by scraping together a few pennies and buying a bottle of cheap liquor. Otherwise the family's annual diversion is limited to *Onam*, the four-day harvest festival at which all the villagers wear new clothes and sing and dance day and night in what one of them calls a glorious celebration.

Shortly after his marriage Krishnankutty obtained a job as a coolie building a highway on the India-China border for the Indian government. The job lasted for only a year and Krishnankutty returned home to work in the fields for thirty cents a day. "Why are you starving down there?" his older brother asked him one day. "Come up and cultivate the land near me." The brother had been given five acres of government forest land as a gratuity for military service. The land had not been properly surveyed, so the brothers extended the plot by half an acre and Krishnankutty moved his growing family to their new home. He cleared the land and planted tapioca and since he couldn't exist on half an acre he went into the forest, marked off an acre and began to cultivate it.

The man sat across the table from me, his fingers playing with a glass of brandy as he talked quietly of violence. Outside the café Sunday afternoon traffic was light on the streets of Caracas, the modern capital of Venezuela. There was no sign of the police round-up, going on at that very moment, of Communist demonstrators who a few days earlier had been bombing the American embassy and rioting against the democratically elected Betancourt government. "I'm sorry that I couldn't take part in those riots," the man said, "but I was in Cuba at the time." For the next several hours he maintained this matter-of-fact tone, though his brown, steel eyes gave away his emotion over events that had seared his innermost feelings.

Aristides Bastidas is a thirty-seven-year-old father of two children, science reporter for the daily *El Nacional*, secretary general of the National Union of Press Workers, and card-carrying Communist. He is a short, stocky man with a look of weariness on his face; his clothes are a little rumpled and his hair mussed. He writes well and the previous year had received a national newspaper award for his science reporting. Everything about him reveals a life of hardship.

Bastidas was born of farming parents in the village of San Pablo, 180 miles west of Caracas, in barren land rising gently to the mountains. His father was one of two thousand *campesinos* who rented a patch of land from a wealthy landowner. Half of each man's crop of corn and black beans had to be returned to the owner. His family lived in a three-room hut made of wood and baked mud. The floor was cement and cardboard walls separated the rooms. Water was obtained at a public well where pigs and burros, as well as humans, came to drink. Aristides was the eldest of three.

"The landowners never got to know the poor people," Bastidas told me. "They would go to Caracas and then to Europe and then come back to their homes. They lived in another world. They wouldn't even go to mass in the church with us, but would go to a private chapel on some landowner's estate. My family was literally starving on sterile land. I had to get out and help them and the only place that looked promising for us was Caracas. When I told the priest that we were leaving, he indicated that, well, he would have one less problem. I guess when you have a thousand flies buzzing around you and one leaves you don't really notice that it's gone."

The shack on the edge of the cemetery that became the family's home in Caracas was worse by far than the one they had left. His father found work as a labourer in the sewage system, while the mother contributed to the family income by making *arepas*, a ground corn food, and selling them in neighbourhood *bodegas*.

Bastidas had a variety of jobs as he continued his education in the first year of high school but when he was fifteen his father, who was forty-one, died of overwork and poor food. Even though Aristides went to work full time, the problem of bare existence for the family became almost insuperable. As he looks back now he comments, "There was an erosion in the belief as well as the practice of my faith. There was just enough time to stay alive."

He got a job as a guard in a psychiatric hospital (he still carries the scar of a seventeen-inch wound suffered when an inmate threw a pot at him), and here he took his first step in union activities. He organized the nurses and guards, who were badly treated by the management, into a union. At the age of sixteen Bastidas was its president but the government outlawed the union and Bastidas was sent to jail, the first of several sentences.

This was the turning point in his life: "In jail I met Communists who were political prisoners. They were great fighters for agrarian reform. I began to see Communism as a solution to the misery of the people I knew. I was young and scared then, but the Communists befriended me. The next year I joined the Party. I didn't know much about it but I began to read and study."

❧❀❧

When I was in Nigeria I made a special trip to Owerri, in the heart of the Ibo territory on the east side of the country, to meet James

Ibole. I had been introduced by mail to him by one of his tribesmen Mark Mere, whom I had met in New York. Mere was a student in education at Fordham University and his family and mine had become friends. He was anxious for me to meet his relatives in Nigeria. Ibole ceremoniously presented a *kola* nut to me, a symbol of acceptance and friendship.

Ibole, forty-four, was a teacher. He and his wife Theresa, forty-one, had nine children aged twenty-three to four. One of the daughters was married and the other eight children lived with their parents in a compound. Although their mud and clay house is small, it doesn't hinder family activities which are carried on for the most part out of doors. Behind the main house, containing a living room surrounded by four bedrooms, is a cookhouse where the family's staple diet of beans, yams and ground corn are cooked over a fire of twigs and sticks. Ibole's teaching salary is $200 a year. The family income is augmented by Mrs. Ibole who sells vegetables every day in a nearby market.

By Owerri standards the family is reasonably prosperous. By the standards of the West they have few possessions indeed. Water must be hauled a half mile. There is no electricity. Ironing is done with a coal iron. Yet a pristine joy shines through Ibole's family life.

The day begins at 5:30 a.m. in the Ibole compound. Each child has assigned tasks of cleaning the compound and washing dishes after breakfast, which is eaten in informal style. Unlike many African women, Theresa Ibole does not seem harried and has time to talk with and enjoy her children. The younger children have few toys and spend their time playing in a nearby field. The eldest girl Juliana, a teacher, is romantically interested in a young man but doesn't like to see him too often because they aren't engaged. Ibole's recreation consists mainly in teaching which gives him more satisfaction, he says, than attending political meetings: "I have much happiness compared with the little bit I do for God."

❧

When I now read the volumes of statistics and abstract reports about the gigantic economic and social problems in the world, I think about these problems in the human terms of Krishnankutty,

Bastidas and Ibole. It is one thing to read about poverty in a far-off land; it is another to see it in the eyes of a man in his own home.

I lived in the United States during these years of travel and discovery and when I returned to Canada in 1965 I had to rediscover my homeland. I had to try to relate the second-largest country in the world, a land of vast resources and potential, to a new world coming into existence, an exploding world of millions of people who shared the same hopes and fears, griefs and anxieties as Krishnankutty, Bastidas and Ibole.

The Canada I came back to was beginning to discover the meaning of future shock. That very phrase, now so much a part of our vocabulary, would have seemed like Orwellian material in the passive, secure Canada in which I grew up.

❦

As a boy I used to lie in bed listening to the sturdy resonance of the bell in the Peace Tower in Ottawa as it pealed the hours. That was thirty-five years ago and we lived about a mile from Parliament Hill. Sandy Hill was a nice, convenient place to live, but now our modest house has been torn down to make way for the expanding University of Ottawa. It gives me a strange feeling to see my eldest daughter dashing into the university library that now dominates "my street."

It was a peaceful, shady street. I remember bread and milk and ice being delivered by horse-drawn carts. We never seemed to mind the mess the horses made on the street. We just took life for granted —of course, that's the boy speaking. My parents must have worried about the bills in those depression years, but they never revealed their worries, at least not before the children.

Around the corner was the church or, more accurately, two huge churches, both of them Roman Catholic—one for the English-speaking, the other for the French. United in faith, divided in language. Separate but equal. St. Joseph's was our church and it was like a second home for me (it wasn't that I prayed that much—there were parish tennis courts beside the church and socials in the parish hall). Priests were frequent visitors in our home and the religious atmosphere provided its own kind of security. The parish missions, Forty Hours devotions, candlelight processions on Christmas Eve. Catholic faith and Catholic culture. The two were so intertwined they were as one. Sandy Hill was a village, serene and passive.

Narrow or confining? I don't recall ever thinking that. I never wanted to rebel against a restrictive upbringing because I was never conscious that it was restrictive. I looked upon the Church as having all the answers but that was before I began to ask tough questions. There was not only a harmony in my life but a steady infusion of values about right and wrong. Answers, security and salvation were all wrapped up in a neat package called life. As I look back on those formative years, I can see that my faith in God, and by extension the Church, made me feel good about myself. What anxieties I had stemmed from a decidedly modest ability in sports but my self-esteem usually bounced back when I concentrated on school journalism.

Only later did the disharmony and injustices of the world shake my complacency and dependence on faith and Church to provide solutions. The Church would go through its own metamorphosis in a culturally exploding world and so would I. The first hints of this occurred when I was nineteen and went to Europe for the summer of 1949. The ravages of war were still widespread. I felt awkward being a tourist in countries where people were rebuilding their basic lives. I spent a lot of time in Rome and though the churches and museums filled me with the traditional awe, I began to feel the excessive cultural conformity of the clerical church.

This was my first stage in a new spiritual perception. Nothing profound or instant. Just a gradual enlarging of my horizons over the next few years. I went to work writing obituaries for the local newspaper (my biography describes this period as the beginning of my journalistic career). Then I went back to college and That Girl became a preoccupation. We went to church together—dances too —and had great college years. I founded a yearbook, announced a contest for the best title, named it *The Best Years* and gave myself the prize.

Marriage, babies, bills, job changes. The familiar pattern. My thinking was still conditioned by the formalized world I had come out of, not yet open to what lay ahead. I was still in my twenties then, restless and not knowing what I really wanted. I was attracted by religious journalism and the United States looked interesting, so off we went. And then came the 60s. Bittersweet years in which I finally broke out of the Catholic culture and grasped the meaning of my faith in deeper terms. My life shifted into a larger arena and it was there that I discovered the relationship of Christianity to the human condition.

Obviously this discovery of the fullness of Christianity was not a one-man effort. The whole world was suddenly in upheaval and every old value seemed to come under attack. Pope Pius XII was dead and there was a new man, with the loving smile of a grandfather, standing at the open papal window with his arms outstretched to the world. Pope John, a very human, believable man. John F. Kennedy's religious sophistication made me—and millions of his electors—respond creatively to Pope John's idea that "here on earth God's work must truly be our own." The technological revolution, the cultural upheaval, religious experimentation; little by little, book by book, person by person, I was reaching out.

I was lucky in the 60s because I travelled a lot and kept making personal discoveries. It was a shock to walk though the Church of the Holy Sepulchre in Jerusalem, built on the very spot where Christ died that all may be one in Him, and see the denominations squabbling over rights to the church. I spent a morning walking through the Garden of Gethsemane by myself. It was there that the ridiculous tragedy of Christian division hit me full in the face. I went to Africa, Latin America and India, and the non-white, non-western world opened up to me. A world of much suffering and culture and pride. I made the amazing discovery that the white, western world is by no means superior in the family of man. For a moment I could see from an African or Asian viewpoint how western technology has contributed not only to the liberation but the enslavement of man.

All this was making me more conscious that the separation of faith from social concern, as a hangover from the doctrine of the separation of church and state, was leading religion to irrelevance.

It ought to be the constant value of faith, I thought, that turns a person outward to work for a better human society rather than taking refuge from the complexity of the changing world in the security of belief. What I was looking for was a faith that would help me to see that life itself is a religious practice. I wanted an existence that would end the dichotomy between religion and life, even if that meant giving up the comfort of spiritual security.

It was Pope John who focused in my mind haunting questions about the human condition around us—the poverty, the racial discrimination, the underdeveloped countries. John XXIII is widely remembered for his benign embrace of mankind and for establishing the Second Vatican Council, which turned out to be the most important council in the history of the Church. But just as great an accomplishment was his encyclical *Pacem in Terris* (Peace on Earth) which in the decade following his death provided continuing impetus to the U.S.-based Center for the Study of Democratic Institutions.

Robert M. Hutchins, Center president, recognized it as "one of the most profound and significant documents of our age" and put the Center's Fellows to work analysing its implications for a major turnaround in world affairs. Norman Cousins, the editor of *Saturday Review* who had served in a private capacity as emissary between Pope John, President Kennedy and Nikita Khrushchev during the post-Cuban missile crisis period, said, "Space flights, nuclear energy and all other of modern man's spectacular achievements did not have the impact on history of an eighty-one-year-old man dying of cancer, using the Papacy to make not just his own Church but all Churches fully relevant and fully alive in the cause of human unity and peace."

As Thomas Aquinas had done centuries before him, John XXIII emphasized that peace is the work of charity and justice; it is not merely the absence of war but the nature of human life everywhere. Thus *Pacem in Terris* began appropriately with a list of human rights. Every human being is a person, every person has the right to life, to bodily integrity, to food, clothing, shelter, rest, medical care and social services, to security in case of sickness, inability to work, widowhood, old age, unemployment or deprival otherwise of the means of subsistence through no fault of his own. Everyone has the right to respect for his person, to his good reputation, the right to freedom in searching for truth and in expressing and communicating his opinions, the right to be informed truthfully about public events, the right to share in the benefits of culture. Everyone has the right to a basic education and to suitable technical and professional training, the right to free initiative in the economic field and the right to work under good working conditions with a proper, just and sufficient wage. Finally, everyone has the right to private property with its accompanying social duties, the rights of residence and freedom of movement, of membership in the human family and the world communities.

With this sweeping document providing a blueprint for humanity John consigned nuclear arms, nationalism, colonialism, racism and non-constitutional regimes to the wastebaskets of history. He asserted that "the same moral law which governs relations between individual human beings serves also to regulate the relations of political communities with each other."

Although this moral thunderclap appeared to die away in the new age of accelerating events, it has provided a basis for four convocations held by the Center for the Study of Democratic Institutions to determine how the principles of *Pacem in Terris* could be put into practice. (The third of these seminars drew five thousand persons who gathered in Washington, D.C. in 1973 to hear foreign policy discussed by a long list of political luminaries headed by Henry Kissinger.)

The encyclical had been addressed not to Catholics alone but to all men of good will. For the old ways of a church speaking only to itself were no longer sufficient. The key idea in *Pacem in Terris*— the need for a human community under law—is the dominant imperative of twentieth-century man. Far from being remote or detached from the hard realities of world struggle, John knew where these realities were pointing. He expounded not only a new vision of humanity but attainable goals. Beyond the stress and clamour of nationalities there must be created a viable new form of world organization with authority to regulate the dealings among nations under justice and law. With all his gentleness there was yet the forceful message that the ethics of Christianity could not be separated from the crisis involving the human family.

Although John died shortly after publication of the encyclical, his ideas found their way into a document that was a cornerstone of the Second Vatican Council. Even as the direction of the Council passed into the hands of John's successor, Paul VI, the Johannine principle that Christianity should be an effective witness and servant in the world was reaffirmed. When the four-year Council concluded in 1965, the "Constitution of the Church in the Modern World" was one of its major achievements. It was not a manifesto of specific answers to each of the world's ills but a pastoral message that the Church should put its ideas and values at the service of the human family. The distinguished Protestant theologian Robert McAfee Brown praised the "positive attitude" toward the world evident in the document.

Of course, the ensuing torment and conflict within the Catholic Church as it struggled with the pressures of internal polarization obscured this shift from introspection to dynamic social thinking. But the groundwork had been laid by Pope John and the Council that would guide many people.

I spent a lot of time as a journalist at the Vatican Council. The more I studied it the less concerned I became with institutional trivia and the more I wanted to see the development of social justice programs, embracing all believers who would act as powerful conscience and critics of the social ills of the world. If I was already in the process of escaping the bonds of a narrow Catholic culture in order to discover the universal meaning of the faith, the Vatican Council was the instrument that codified the process.

The deeper into the Council I plunged, the more I could see that faith belonged on main street—not the evangelical, street-corner witness faith (at least for me), but as an identification with the social process in the community and hence a chance to participate in the input into the value system. Elementary? Perhaps for some. But for me it had to be a long journey from the sanctuary of Sandy Hill to be able to live with the insecurity of not having all the answers.

With the ideas of Pope John the 1960s dawned with great promise —and the excitement of John F. Kennedy. We stayed up all night when he was elected and his inaugural was like the birth of a new age. Everything began to happen so quickly that every day seemed an adventure. Of everything that has been said about Kennedy, the revisionist and muck-raking schools included, the quality that stands out most in my mind was his ability to sensitize people. He himself was sensitive to the reality of human pain and the fragility of human life and he communicated a sense of reason, creativity and vision that gives civilization its forward movement. He made us feel bigger than we are; that we could rise above saturating trivia and redefine our purpose.

This quality of sensitivity is extremely rare in leaders in any field. Pope John had it along with Kennedy, which might explain why it is so hard to think of any other leaders who have enjoyed such universal appeal in recent times.

I remember the day I spent in the Indian parliament in New Delhi listening to a raucous argument between the Speaker and a dissident Member. Later in a plane I happened to sit beside one of the Members who had taught school while studying law so that he could embark on a political career. Now he represented one million people and he talked happily about how the gigantic power dams being built by the government would better their lives through the irrigation of millions of acres. He spoke gratefully of the five billion dollars that India had received from the United States in foreign aid and predicted that President Kennedy would receive a welcome in India surpassing that which any leader had ever received anywhere. Three days later the Dallas shots reverberated around the world.

There were other forces influencing me also, principally Ghandi, Dietrich Bonhoeffer and Martin Luther King, all of whom gave their lives for the development of a true human brotherhood. They were deeply religious men but they showed us that the world is not something to endure in order to find salvation; rather the world provides the opportunity to complete the work of God's creation. I was beginning to understand that every individual holds within him the power to add to creation, to add to the stature of the world. Jean Vanier, the great Canadian humanitarian who shelters the mentally retarded in France, puts this point very well: "Our lives are fleeting moments in which are found the seeds of eternal peace, unity and love as well as the seeds of war, dissension and indifference. When will we rise and awaken to the choice before each of us, to water and to give light to one or the other of these two seeds?"

When the opportunity arose to return to Canada to be the founding editor of the *Western Catholic Reporter*, a newspaper committed to the ideas of Vatican II, it seemed a natural step to take. I was soon swept up in a new life in Edmonton and spent a lot of time on my return travelling through and rediscovering the Canada I had left nine years earlier.

On my first "voyage of rediscovery" from Vancouver to Halifax I was browsing one day in the Ottawa Public Library and came upon a balding, pudgy chap who greeted me by name. He looked vaguely familiar but I couldn't place him. It took a minute of roundabout conversation before I fixed him in my mind as an old school chum. With an enthusiasm I couldn't recall his having possessed in the past he told me he was taking French lessons and was now passable in the language. He had taken up the piano, was reading Chekhov and relaxed with Shakespeare. "I may be past forty," he said, "but I've got a new supply of energy. I'm getting more out of life than ever before." It occurred to me that my friend personified the spirit of modern Canada—the qualities of zest, culture and a new-found determination that I had been encountering, yet not fully understanding, in our national life.

Just as I had failed to recognize my friend, I had failed until that moment to understand how deeply run the currents of the new Canadian spirit. Now the new civic pride, the frenzy of culture, the awakened interest in religion, the facing up to the demands of multiculturalism and the attitude of get-up-and-go all came into sharper focus.

The evidence was everywhere. I saw a beautiful university, built in the Grecian concept, carved on top of a mountain overlooking Vancouver; a towering cylindrical city hall in Toronto, an architectural fantasy; Place Ville Marie in Montreal, a complex of glittering needle-like buildings, underground shops and noon-hour theatre that have made a civilized community out of an urban crossroads; a new cultural centre in Ottawa, which I used to regard as the most culturally deprived capital in the western world; skyscrapers on the prairies; arching bridges, superhighways galore; and almost everywhere I turned, new schools, churches, shopping centres and homes.

The physical transformation of the land was the most dramatic sign of our new strength. The quickening development of natural resources (even if aided by American capital) was unlocking the door to the future: the St. Lawrence Seaway, Alberta oil, Saskatchewan potash and enough untapped minerals to make us dizzy in contemplation (the meaning of the energy crisis was still to come).

I revelled in the simple discoveries I was making about the strength and advantages of Canadians compared with what I had seen in so many countries elsewhere. Our freedom from political oppression is taken for granted, yet oppression is widespread around the globe. We have poverty undeniably but it does not dominate our national life. Our wheat, lumber and mines have made us rich. Our political heritage has given us a democracy that, for all its faults, respects the human person. Here we are free to follow our consciences and seek our spiritual destiny. We are not a perfect society but here is found all the opportunity that most people can handle in a lifetime.

As we turned the corner into our centennial year nagging thoughts kept interrupting my reverie about our great accomplishments. I started to look more closely at our own political process. The year of our centennial and Expo had about it the air of national purpose but as the 70s began we seemed to revert as a people to a preoccupation with ourselves. The domestic economy. Bilingual relations. New social programs. Having built and stabilized this country, I wondered, would Canadians now look outward to the majority of mankind that still struggles for the livelihood that we take for granted?

I found myself being invited to speak in many places across Canada. The invitations that pleased me the most came from the

Protestant and Anglican churches in my own community. I told my listeners how important Christian reconciliation was for me and the response I received was consistently warmer than that which I felt with Catholic audiences. Deep friendships blossomed from these inter-Christian contacts.

The ideas of Pope John, Ghandi, Vanier and other humanitarians poured out of me in articles and speeches. I tried to depict a world caught up in revolutionary change: instant communications, ten hours' travel to anywhere, the tearing down of racial, religious and cultural barriers. In this new world military hardware will not be the guarantor of national safety; rather, people will come to understand that it is the economic development of those vast areas of the earth now containing poverty-stricken millions that will fulfil our legitimate aspirations. When we understand that a homeless family, an unemployed provider, a hungry child anywhere on earth prevents peace, then we will see the futility of trying to achieve peace without helping the millions who cannot keep up with the changing world.

∽✣∾

I never sat down and wrote out a great political manifesto. There was no blinding moment of inspiration. Rather I had cross currents in my mind about so much of our national political effort being devoted to reacting to technological fallout when a new sense of direction and leadership in a changing world should be our chief priority. Despite our progress, public cynicism was replacing belief and hope in a better society and a better world. Why? What was going wrong?

The more I looked at this question the more I became convinced that our priorities are wrong. But in the spirit of universality found among youth I saw signs of hope for a more human world. In the new generation we see a growing interest in the common good of mankind and in the brotherhood of all men. If McLuhan's "global village" has moved beyond a concept anywhere, it is in those, principally the young, who feel themselves members of a new race— that of citizens of the world.

One day in Ottawa I went for a walk around Parliament Hill, as my wife Eva and I had done so often in the past. I sat on a bench and thought it all over. I was in my early forties, I wanted to move my ideas into a national forum, the Progressive Conservatives were the only party that appealed to me and I thought I could win my home constituency of Edmonton-Strathcona.

Back in Edmonton Eva and I weighed the pros and cons of political life—especially with Parliament two thousand miles away from our home. The disruption in our family life was easy enough to forecast but only experience would indicate our ability to cope with it.

Evita, our eldest child, was then sixteen and just starting college at the University of Ottawa where she had been awarded a scholarship. Getting elected would enable us to live together so that seemed a plus. Our second daughter, Mickey, then fourteen, is severely mentally retarded and had just entered St. Joseph's Hospital in Edmonton. Doug, twelve, Mary Anne, ten, and Patti, eight, all concerned me because at that age they needed their father around. Still, I felt they were good kids with sound values and so busy during the week with their sports, music and drama interests that they would not miss me greatly. And I would be home on weekends. Quality would make up for quantity in time spent with them. At least that was the way I theorized.

Eva, a social worker, had only recently rejoined her profession after many years out of it while the children were small. She was acquiring a professional reputation in the community and I wanted to foster it, not make her start all over again in Ottawa. As in the past Eva was agreeable to moving. But both of us concluded that our life in Edmonton meant a great deal to us. I knew I would feel less guilty commuting to Ottawa knowing that Eva was happy in her developing career in early childhood education.

All of this would be making the best of a decision—to enter politics—once made. As for the decision itself, I was as usual becoming preoccupied with an idea building within me and not wanting to think too much of the negative aspects. Just the idea that as an ordinary, decidedly unwealthy person I might be able to walk onto the floor of the House of Commons set my mind buzzing with the strategy of how to do it. Eva, anticipating better than I the human scramble of the next few years, was not enthusiastic. But she knew from past experience that I wanted a green light.

I prepared myself mentally for a lot of weekend flying.

It seemed natural for me to gather together one afternoon fifteen clergymen of various denominations to get their reactions and advice about my political involvement. They represented all political leanings but they were united in their desire to sensitize people to modern social problems. We talked a lot about the dynamics of social change today and how spiritual values need to be re-examined and expressed in a modern idiom. We explored the difficulty of getting nominated and elected. They were by no means sure that I could do it. Some thought I wasn't tough enough. But there was a consensus that I ought to try.

As we got up to leave, Ed Checkland, an erudite and slightly acerbic Baptist minister, put his hand on my shoulder: "I hope you don't get swallowed up by that big machine in Ottawa."

❧ 2 ❧

THE ME NOBODY KNOWS

"I'm Frank McMillan and I hear you want to run for Parliament."

The voice over the phone was strong, aggressive and with that one sentence I knew the individual would turn out to be dynamic. Frank McMillan became the cornerstone of my political career— the man who gave me political confidence and devised the early strategy for my election.

I needed McMillan because I had no political organization. In fact, having made the decision to run for Parliament I discovered that I scarcely knew anybody in the Canadian political world. I had once had lunch with Robert Stanfield on one of his visits to Edmonton but our conversation was on national topics and I wasn't thinking about local politics at the time. The only other person at the lunch was Joe Clark, then an executive assistant to Mr. Stanfield, now leader of the Party.

I later decided to talk to Clark about the prospects in my home constituency, Edmonton-Strathcona. If I was going to run it would be with the Conservatives, I told Clark. Not that I had a deep political ideology. I just thought that Stanfield and his politics would stop the endless proliferation of bureaucracy and restore in Canadians a sense of personal initiative and pride in participating in the development of Canada. I resented the superiority of the Liberal administration and strongly opposed two policy decisions: to pay farmers not to grow wheat and to fight inflation by allowing unemployment to rise. I felt that I would be more at home, and perhaps more personally creative, with the Conservatives.

Strathcona was then held by Hu Harries, a Liberal who w.
puted to be a man of great intelligence, at intellectual odds
Trudeau and, more important from an Opposition standpoin
Member who did not go to Parliament very often. He had won the
seat in the Trudeau sweep of 1968 by defeating a ten-year House
veteran Terry Nugent, a Conservative and Diefenbaker loyalist.
Since his defeat Nugent had allowed the Conservative organization
to become almost moribund.

I had never met Harries or Nugent so I decided to do my own
random survey throughout the constituency on both men. I started
finding out who the politically astute people were and knocked on
their doors. I called on a variety of people not involved in politics.
After about two weeks of these conversations my findings pointed
to a double conclusion: the Conservatives wanted a new candidate;
that candidate would win the seat.

I compiled a list of about one hundred people I or my wife knew in
the constituency—some well, most vaguely—and wrote them letters
asking if they would support my candidacy for the nomination.
About thirty people responded, ten in a way that indicated they were
willing to work.

Frank McMillan's name was not on the original list. Ruth Wallace,
a friend of my wife, received my letter shortly after this gregarious
men's wear representative set up a sample room across the hall from
her office. Chatting with him, she learned that he had just come
from Calgary and was interested in politics. She gave him my letter.

McMillan came to see me and within an hour I knew he was the
man to organize my political life. Young, straight-talking, fashion-
ably dressed, he was the embodiment of the new-style politics then
coming into vogue in Alberta. The province was about to have an
election which was called for August 30, 1971. We decided to become involved in our respective provincial constituencies so that
we would learn something about campaigning and meet people who
might later work for us. I signed on as official agent for Julian
Koziak, a young lawyer running with Lougheed's Conservatives
against the incumbent Minister of Lands and Forests. McMillan
went to work for Don Getty, a rising political star in Alberta. Both

of us were learning on the job. We often toured various campaign headquarters around Edmonton, looking for ideas, seeing what worked, what didn't—and more important, who worked. It was in Koziak's campaign that I soon began to observe an assistant named Shona Wehm who had the great facility of not only getting to know everyone but getting them to take on jobs.

Koziak and Getty won handsomely in the Lougheed provincial victory. McMillan and I had a list of workers and a knowledge of modern procedures. We asked Shona to join us as coordinator. Since a federal election in 1972 appeared certain, we wanted an early nomination to give us more time to build up Roche, an unknown candidate. The first goal was to get a nomination meeting called and to obtain that, there would have to be a meeting of the Strathcona Progressive Conservative Association. I went to the president, told him I wanted to run, asked for a meeting and took away some membership tickets to sell. He was not enthusiastic about having a nomination meeting but after a few follow-up phone calls, he assembled his executive and they agreed to an association meeting on September 22. That was all McMillan and I needed.

We figured thirty-five people would be enough to carry the vote our way without tipping our hand that we had a lot more than that to bring out to the nomination meeting. True to our calculations about sixty people showed up for the September 22 meeting. One of our supporters moved that a nomination meeting be held November 8. Nugent argued against it, since he would have a better chance for the nomination if it were held after the election had been called. Our side won handily. We ordered five hundred membership cards, called a meeting of twenty of our most enthusiastic supporters, prepared a small brochure listing my few political assets and started building larger lists of people.

I had been reading books on political theory and manuals that fascinated me. But I became convinced that it all boiled down to two basic rules: keep the nucleus around you small and don't peak too soon. The group around me was small: Darryl Smith, Phil Arlette, Diane Rehill, Woody Johnson—and McMillan and Shona. We proceeded on the pyramid theory—one person would lead to two more and they would be sold by personal contact. Coffee parties would be the vehicle.

We set a budget of $1,000 and I insisted that all of it would have to be raised. Not only could I not afford the money myself but I wanted to prove that a candidate could be nominated and elected without spending a cent of his own. I thought this would be a good instance of principle and pragmatism going together.

McMillan and I went to the first coffee party. It was a disaster. We were the first to arrive. Only half the invited guests showed up and the half dozen who came seemed more interested in advancing the N.D.P. cause than in hearing a Conservative position. We were fast learners. After that we drew up rules for hostesses. We wanted a crowded room, coffee served before we arrived, thirty minutes for presentation and questions, a second serving of coffee, allowing me to stand up and circulate while my colleague sold $2 membership and impressed on recipients the necessity of coming to the November 8 meeting in order to nominate Doug Roche.

The coffee parties started moving well. Often guests volunteered to be hostesses. We wrote everyone who signed up, kept in touch with them by phone, held back reporting new members to the executive until the deadline. Nugent was running. So were two other candidates, both for the first time, Don Axford and Chuck Cripps. McMillan, a great believer in projecting an air of victory no matter what's happening, ordered buttons, balloons and a band to lead me into the nomination meeting. Two nights before the nomination he had a party for the workers at his house and asked me to come late. He was finishing his pep talk as I arrived and when I stepped into the living room everyone applauded. It was the first time I had the feeling of people believing in me, looking to me. He had brought the campaign to a peak. That night we knew we could beat anybody.

I had my speech ready: "To be alive today is to feel the birth of a new era in history. . . . We live simultaneously in the Age of Aquarius and the Age of Anxiety. . . . Further technological and scientific advances will be of no avail unless we can develop the moral capacity to utilize them constructively for the benefit of all men. . . . To create or to despair, that is our choice. . . ." But speeches are not important at nominations, supporters are. We had 515 of the 799 voters on the first ballot.

We were then plugged into the P.C. election material for candidates but Frank, Shona and I prepared our own plan of action and drew up a budget of $25,000, most of it for advertising. We kept our nucleus small. Bob Lloyd took on the demanding task of raising money, a job made all the more difficult by the fact that he was promoting an unknown. Harold Alston, a United Church minister and communications teacher, began shooting film of my activities for T.V. commercials which turned out to be professional knockouts. Fil Fraser, a broadcaster and film-maker, decided to do a one-hour movie on the campaign right up to election day (which was later shown on the CBC) and he began attending our strategy sessions for background. After the election Fraser told me his working title of the film had been "Nice Guys Finish Last."

The campaign, of course, had to be kept in low gear until the election was actually called. When the possibility of a June election went by, McMillan warned me that he would not be able to manage a fall campaign because it would conflict with his business bookings throughout the province. Finally the Prime Minister set the date for October 30. When I assembled the nucleus, now numbering about thirty, our whole program was ready and confidence filled the campaign headquarters. I asked Darryl Smith to manage the campaign as well as the media advertising. McMillan drove me hard but Smith relaxed me and I could see that over the sixty-day period I would probably survive better under Smith. I became convinced of this when I introduced a lady to Darryl whom I thought was the convention manager of a Calgary hotel—and she turned out to be Darryl's wife. "Well, now you know what a brilliant politician you have on your hands," I told Darryl. Instead of making me feel more uncomfortable, he laughed at my gaffe. I felt so badly that I later went out and bought a rose for Bernice Smith.

Intensive door-to-door coverage of as many of the 282 polls as I could manage, tours of shopping centres and coffee parties were the key elements in the campaign. Get to as many people as possible personally.

The first of the 9,000 doors I knocked on startled me. "Can I talk to you about the federal election, sir?" I asked a middle-aged man. "No," he said and shut the door. Was this what door-to-door was like? It was not. Generally I found people friendly and receptive. I had runners moving ahead of me down the block so I would not lose time by waiting for people to answer. Just a hello, a handshake, quick communication. Initial impression. A man on the run. Forty seconds per door, say the manuals. Very few people asked me what I stood for. To those who did ask I responded that I would send them my position papers and I gave these names and addresses every night to the campaign office staff.

"Doug Roche's Ideas and Commitments" was the name of the document I had prepared during the summer. This took the form of ten one-page outlines giving the situation, the goal and steps to the goal on these subjects: the right to a job and stable prices; Edmonton, pivot for the north and Pacific; pay people, not governments; stronger Parliament means better government; economic independence, accentuate the positive; a combined voice for Strathcona; the big global cleanup; Canada's role in world peace; multiculturalism: a valuable plant; national unity: helping everyone "plug in."

In the introduction I tried to set out my philosophy of government as succinctly as possible:

> I believe that the federal government today is too big, too dominant, too expensive and imposes itself too much in people's lives. The policies of the present administration are making too many people overly dependent on government; those who truly need protection are hurt in the process.
>
> I believe in strong institutions in our society as the best protection of people's freedom. The weakening of Parliament by the present government has contributed to the breakdown in respect for our institutions. Just as we cannot have education without schools, law without courts and justice without jails, we cannot have good government without a strong Parliament. We live in a time of exciting change and new possibilities and Parliament must show that it is responsive to people's needs if people are to continue to believe in it.

I thought the next few sentences risked being dismissed as rhetoric but I used them because they expressed how I truly felt:

> I believe that the cornerstone of public policy in Canada today must be the rights and dignity of the individual human being. That is the principle against which I will test public policies. That is the principle that will restore trust between the people and the federal government. That is the principle that will reinvigorate Canada with economic prosperity, human freedom and national independence.

I used the position papers as the basis of my comments at all-candidate forums where I met my competitors and studied their styles: Hu Harries seeking re-election for the Liberals, who appeared to me to talk down to people; Howard Leeson for the N.D.P., a young, personable political science instructor who was undoubtedly sincere in his convictions and who would do well in siphoning off the anti-Liberal vote; Bill Pelech for the Social Credit, a teacher who used every opening to expound on convoluted Socred theory; two angry girls from the university running under different communist labels who regularly vented their hostility on the audiences.

Most people who go to forums are committed to a party or candidate. Very few are swayed by what they hear. That's what the experts say and I think they're right. Local candidates win because they are part of a national wind blowing or because they somehow get through to enough individual voters who then identify with the person whose name they will put an "X" beside.

One of the best pieces of political advice I received was from a retiring politician who said to get off the stage fast at public forums, get to the back of the hall first and shake hands with as many people as possible on the way out. Often I would notice my competitors talking to the handful of people who always come to the stage after an event is over to discuss points in detail with speakers—while I was at the back of the room shaking hands with perhaps two hundred people, looking them in the eye and asking them to vote for me.

The countdown began to pick up speed. From my diary:

Day 46.   Business calls with Marcel Perras in morning. Belgravia poll with Art Brotheridge in afternoon. Poll 7 with Sid Jeffels in evening. Media meeting with Darryl at 10 p.m., followed by organizational meeting for Stanfield rally.

Day 19.   8 a.m. budget conference with Lloyd, Johnson, Smith. Organizing remaining polls to be covered in time available. Forum at College St. Jean at 3:30 followed immediately with door-to-door with Laurie Halferdahl in low-rise apartment area until 8. Home to change for coffee party at Jackie Phillips'. 10:15 conference with Smith and Dave Kilgour on election day program.

Day 11.   Business calls in morning. Harry Ainlay school forum 12-1:20 p.m. (D. R. wins straw vote). Duggan polls in afternoon with Hugh Campbell. Dinner at 5 p.m. Shopping centre tour with Cy Turner 6-8:30 p.m. Coffee parties, 8:30 at Emily Rowan's, 9:30 at Elaine Stewart's.

Day 5.   Budget meeting 7:30 a.m. with Lloyd, Johnson. Open line CJCA 9-10:45 a.m. Speech at luncheon, Rotary Club. Visit to Pensioners Concerned open house. Forum and visit at Good Samaritan Hospital. Appearance at Marian Centre annual dinner. Speech to Business and Professional Women's Society at Mayfair Hotel. Coffee party sponsored by Mrs. Murray in party room at Varscona Towers attended by 120 people. 10 p.m. election day meeting with Smith, Kilgour until midnight.

One of the greatest favours the media do for candidates is to make them pay in advance for advertisements. If you don't have the money you don't spend it—and you don't get a bill thirty days later. Bob Lloyd and Woody Johnson had promised me that I would not wake up the morning after the election—win or lose—owing money to anybody. I trusted them completely. Lloyd and his team provided 203 cash contributions averaging $90. The Progressive Conservative central fund put $10,000 into our campaign. A few firms loaned us equipment. Johnson proved to be a tough treasurer, the kind I respect. His favourite word was "no" to requests to spend more money. We could see the expenses going over $25,000 but Johnson and I drew the absolute limit at $30,000 (which would include the carry-over nomination debt and work out to 43 cents per voter). Just as I never worried about the outcome of the election, I never worried about our ability to raise money.

I have often said after the election that I owed nothing to any one person—except that I owed everything to so many. By election day Darryl had 900 people involved in large and small ways in the campaign.

Forty-five minutes after the polls closed, Hu Harries phoned to say he hoped I would enjoy "all those Air Canada flights." He had defeated Terry Nugent by 6,000 votes in 1968 and he apparently thought throughout the campaign that this would be enough of a cushion for him, despite Trudeau's declining popularity in the West. But our samplings were sounder and we knew he was beaten from the opening of the campaign. We won 250 of the 282 polls and received a total of 26,908 votes. Harries collected 16,625. Leeson tripled his predecessor's total and received 9,098 votes, by far the best N.D.P. showing in the province.

❧

On my study door at home I have pinned up the cover of a play-bill from a play I once saw in New York, "The Me Nobody Knows."

Five years ago if someone had told me all the things I would do to organize and campaign, I would have responded, "Not me." I did not think I had the personality for the job, I did not want to smile for the sake of smiling, and as for going up to a door and asking someone to vote for me, I would rather have tried for the four-minute mile.

But when I felt the pull inside me to at least try for Parliament, I decided there would have to be a professional Me to complement and protect the personal Me. The personal Me would rather go for walks alone, spend a week in a monastery, read a book, play with my children. The professional Me goes into a crowded room and shakes hands; projects myself to an audience and shrugs off rebuffs by refusing to let them touch my interior.

It's the same Me basically. Not Jekyll and Hyde. The two Me's are different sides of the same person that enable me to be outgoing when I have to be and introspective when I want to be. The latter gives me the strengh to put myself out on the edge, to go where the people are. Where people are is out in the world, working, suffering, loving, hoping. They are not in my study.

I do not mean that I must be phony or make a great effort in meeting people. Most people I meet in my political activities I like. I especially enjoy listening to them. But I feel they don't really know me.

I won my first election not because of my beliefs or philosophy of life and government. I never covered up my thoughts but not very many people were interested in my fundamental beliefs. I won because I was a credible Conservative candidate and as I had predicted two years earlier, a credible Conservative candidate—of any name— would win Edmonton-Strathcona. I won because a lot of people were voting against Trudeau, against Harries, against "Ottawa." Many were voting for Stanfield, for the Conservatives.

How could they have been voting for Doug Roche when hardly anyone knew more than a few basic facts about me? Yet I was given the legal right to walk into the House of Commons and vote according to how I saw the issues. Or was I? Capital punishment, abortion, bilingualism were over the horizon, waiting their turn to force me to come to grips with the classic parliamentary question of whether I was an instrument of popular opinion or a leader.

A newly elected M.P. may come out of an election on an emotional high but he's quickly brought down to earth on entering Parliament—only one of 264 successful people, all as aggressive and ambitious as he is. I could not accept it at first but as the months went by I realized that Parliament is a bruising collision game. Your ideas have to withstand not just attack but being totally ignored.

Thus new M.P.s try to establish their place in the sun. Some so that they will be publicly recognized for the talent they have, some so that they will be promoted by the party leaders, some so that they will survive the next election, some so that their ideas can penetrate society. At home you're in the front row but in Parliament you're one of the crowd—and why should anybody listen to you?

Gradual acceptance by your colleagues becomes the key. Do your homework. Show up for meetings. Routine, but not oblivion. Always the balance. When to speak, when to shut up. When to push an idea, when to forget it. The art of compromise. That's what they call politics. They ought to call it survival in a mixmaster. Then, survival for what? To react or to influence?

I spent a lot of my first year learning how to combine my purposes with the reality of the world. It is important to be noticed. Thus I welcomed the headlines at home when I accused the Prime Minister of playing patronage politics by inviting defeated Liberal candidates to dinner with the Queen and ignoring elected M.P.s. Even though I am a monarchist, having dinner with the Queen is low on my priority list. But although my outrage had a synthetic quality, protests like this build political capital at home. Publicity results in invitations to speak which then enable you to put across your ideas. In the same way, servicing constituents' needs makes you a stronger politician as well as filling genuine needs. If a politician does not keep building political capital, what little he has quickly erodes. He needs attention not just to feed his ego but to survive to do his job.

What happens, though, when you get hooked, when you start picking issues and making statements just because they are hot items for the press? Attention is intoxicating. If you add to this ideological variety the competition for power and personal fringe benefits within a party, you have the warning given to me by a veteran M.P.: "The real enemies you'll make in your career are in your own party."

I have very mixed feelings about the central preoccupation in politics—power. An incredible amount of nonsense and egotism is expended in its pursuit. It distracts us from our situation and makes us believe that, yes, if only we win then change will occur. But power does not confer purpose. Nonetheless, I nod my head to the convention that says you must have power to accomplish anything. The dilemma: power is a necessary means which too often obscures everything else.

Like many others I am moving along the road to doubt about many of these political axioms. I have reached the point where I doubt the practicality of "pragmatism." You calculate every angle until your head falls off, then make your move and discover that in the intervening thirty seconds all the angles have changed.

I thought I was coming to Parliament to make a difference, if only a small one. Yet the pressure to accommodate myself to the tradition of the institution is strong. So it is important to catch myself and recall that despite our gymnastics in the House the world outside these walls is changing profoundly; it will not wait upon the small-mindedness of our politics as usual.

All of this was in my mind one night when I fired off a piece to the Edmonton *Journal*, responding to what I thought was gratuitous comment about M.P.s sponging off the public. I had come to the conclusion that by concentrating on allegedly hot items, the media was distorting Parliament.

"What kind of men and women are we in the House of Commons?" I asked the editor in support of my argument for more substantive and less peripheral coverage of M.P.s. "What are we doing —or not doing—for the people? What do the people of Edmonton really know about the performance of the Members they have sent to Ottawa?" Instead of being judged on my fighting qualities vis-à-vis Mr. Trudeau, I wrote, "I would much rather be judged—for good or bad—on the ideas in my speeches in the House on social reform, decentralization and Ottawa's failure at intergovernmental relations, which no one at home has heard of."

A few days later the editor Andrew Snaddon, who believes a strong fence ought to separate journalists and politicians, replied with the condescension that editors keep handy in their bag of arguments: "Mr. Roche may feel that his and other utterances of matters of national importance were neglected. Possibly, but as a general rule competent people in our wire services can tell what is new as well as interesting and important in speeches and what has been said before and often."

⟨ 3 ⟩

THE VIEW FROM THE BACKBENCH

November 29, 1973. The day began, as so many do, with a committee meeting. The Parliamentary Committee on Justice and Legal Affairs assembled at 9:30 a.m. in room 371 of the West Block which also serves as the Progressive Conservative caucus room. Pictures of Conservative Prime Ministers, starting with Sir John A. Macdonald, hung on the walls. One of those figures of history, John Diefenbaker, was still with us in this Twenty-ninth Parliament. It seemed he might be here for a long time yet.

It was a grey day with the first hint of winter and as I took my seat at the green-felt table I noticed through the windows the Canadian flag fluttering in the wind. I have never forgotten the thrill I felt when I first saw the red-and-white Maple Leaf flying atop the Peace Tower when I came back to Canada in 1965 after nine years' absence. You can't go home again, Thomas Wolfe said. But I had come back, survived the difficulties of re-adjustment and become the elected representative of 109,125 people.

Now my first year as an M.P. had passed—and with it the initiations, frustrations and crises that newcomers encounter. I was beginning to settle down, accepting the fact that I couldn't be everywhere at once and gradually more willing to admit to myself that the influence of a backbencher in the workings of the government and Parliament is remote at best. Many times in that first year I felt that Parliament was an irrelevant charade out of touch with the complex needs of modern society. Yet Parliament is supposed to be where the country comes together.

Across the table I noticed Madame Albanie Morin from Quebec. A Member with tough, hard-line social views, she was impeccably dressed in a pink suit and purple blouse. Beside her, relaxed and smiling in a black-and-white checked jacket, was Mark MacGuigan, the forty-three-year-old former law professor from Windsor who did a notable job co-chairing the Joint Senate-Commons Committee on the Canadian Constitution. At the head of the table beside the chairman was Heath Macquarrie, cherubic, polished and a political historian of distinction.

Not being a lawyer, I do not sit on the Justice Committee—I had signed up for Health and Social Affairs upon entering Parliament and stuck with it—but I asked to be appointed for this one meeting because of the subject. Three bills were before the Committee, dealing with a proposal for a national mid-winter holiday. I had some strong feelings about the purpose of such a holiday, which I had expressed previously when the matter was debated during Private Member's Hour in the House.

Macquarrie led off the discussion, explaining that his bill would honour Sir John A. Macdonald as the first Prime Minister and "primus inter pares" of the Fathers of Confederation. He chuckled as he tossed out a little dig: "A member of the press gallery reading that said that Macquarrie had a tendency to speak in curlicues. Actually 'primus inter pares' is not a curlicue, but Latin, which indicates that classicism is but another of the many prerequisites not required for our press gallery."

Macquarrie made his case for "some historic nationalism," then gave way to Ed Nelson, a former school teacher from British Columbia, who presented his arguments for calling the holiday Canada Flag Day. The third bill had been sponsored by Sinclair Stevens, a new Toronto Member who was promoting Discovery Day to pay tribute to Canadians of the past who have made significant contributions to such fields as music, literature, business, art, science and public service.

This variety of causes prompted Stuart Leggatt, a young Vancouver lawyer, to suggest facetiously, "Is there any way we could compromise all the bills into something like John A. Macdonald discovers Canada-Flag Day and put them all together on a date that we like and clean up this problem?" The chairman, James Jerome from Sudbury, who was to become Speaker following the 1974 election, replied in the same vein: "We have had some minor things before us like the capital punishment and wiretap bills but now we really have something that we can sink our teeth into."

A committee member usually has ten minutes to question or comment when his turn comes. I decided to concentrate on a comment to get across my belief that we in Parliament should do everything we can to encourage a sense of history among Canadians, especially young Canadians.

"I spent nine years of my life outside Canada," I told the Committee. "I lived in the United States where three of my children were born and it quickly became apparent how dedicated the Americans are, and the American school system is, to inculcate in American children a deep sense of history and patriotism." I argued that the three bills should be reconciled by having a Founders' Day that would take into account the great historical achievements of those who have made Canada what it is. Thus, both Sir John A. and Mr. Pearson, identified with the flag, would be honoured.

It was now 11 o'clock and the chairman wound up the meeting with an invitation to everyone to come back the following week. I knew that I would have to be back in the constituency on the day of the next meeting so I had to content myself with following the reconciliation of the bills second-hand. Ultimately the Committee agreed to recommend to the House that the third Monday of each February be declared Heritage Day and celebrated as a national holiday. Each year the emphasis would be on a different figure from our past who had contributed significantly to our heritage. (Two-and-a-half years passed and there was still no action on this proposal.)

Sinclair Stevens and I walked back together to our offices in the Centre Block. Stevens was policy co-ordinator for the forthcoming national Conservative convention and I used these few minutes to brief him on a paper on government decentralization I had written at Mr. Stanfield's request.

"Decentralization isn't a sexy subject," I told Stevens, "but it's a philosophy that can get Ottawa off the backs of people." I touched on the key points such as constitutional change, spreading out the decision-making process of federal government departments and ways to solidify inter-governmental relations. Stevens seemed interested—but one of his great qualities is that he's interested in everything. I knew that my paper could be found somewhere in the Party machinery, but as we parted on the run, I had no expectations that there would be an early discovery.

I was already late for the next committee meeting which had been scheduled for 11 o'clock so I skipped going to my office, even though I had not yet seen the day's mail, and went instead to room 112-N where the meeting of the Procedure and Organization Committee was just getting underway.

I had joined this Committee a few months earlier because it was launching a study of House rules, especially for the daily Question Period, a forty-minute period during which the Opposition questions the government. By extension the Committee began studying, or at least talking about, almost everything in Parliament connected with procedure. It amounted to a crash course for a new Member.

I remembered the afternoon that Speaker Lamoureux had invited the Committee to his sedate chambers for coffee and a discussion of ways to improve the Question Period. After respectfully waiting until a lot of words had flowed over the coffee cups I summoned up my courage and told the Speaker that the constant popping up and down we had to do to get recognized in Question Period was degrading to Parliament and demoralizing to Members in the back rows. The Speaker listened with an air of keen interest in what I was saying about new methods to ensure an orderly manner of questioners arising. "Can I really be getting through to him this easily?" I asked myself as I wound up my presentation. I left the room with a sense of mission accomplished. Months later I was still popping up and down like everyone else.

Jim Walker, a gentle politician from Toronto, was chairman of the Procedure and Organization Committee but today he was away and the chair was filled by Romeo Leblanc, Prime Minister Trudeau's former press secretary who ran in New Brunswick. Ged Baldwin, a veteran Alberta Conservative and then our House leader, presented a plan to upgrade Private Member's Hour.

A traditional feature of the British parliamentary system, Private Member's Hour creates the illusion of accomplishment. A back-bencher, if he is high enough in the draw, gets an hour devoted to his pet subject. He can present a bill or a motion and speak for twenty minutes. Then supporters of the government rebut him until the hour is concluded. The bill or motion, having been "talked out", goes to the bottom of the list without a vote and nothing is ever heard of it again. Only rarely does the government allow the idea to go to committee—one such example was Jim McGrath's campaign to tighten up television advertising directed to children. Usually a Member has to be content with whatever publicity the idea generates back home, which generally isn't much.

In my moment of glory I had presented a case for upgrading social policy in Canada to the same status as economic planning through the creation of a Social Council of Canada. My wife had been practically alone in the gallery and the House all but deserted. But I was undaunted because I had a Great Idea. To this day only the most assiduous readers of Hansard are aware of my proposal. The press, with the exception of the Edmonton *Journal*, ignored the speech. The *Journal* had four paragraphs back with the want ads and I tend to think that these four paragraphs existed because I sent the paper the speech myself.

Nonetheless, I had some satisfaction a few months later when the Economic Council of Canada urged the development of social indi-cators for a better understanding of the economic-social relationship in such areas as housing, health and the environment. We need a broader framework than just economic, the Council said, to measure the overall well-being of the nation. In other words, the top econo-mists were saying that economic criteria dominate our judgment about the success of society to the detriment of a larger understand-ing of what constitutes the quality of life. I am not under any illusion that my speech calling for integrated economic-social planning in-fluenced the Economic Council; what I was pleased with was the confirmation that I was on the right track. In the budget debate shortly afterward I drew the Finance Minister's attention to the publicly acknowledged need for social indicators in economic planning but drew no response.

All of this was one more reason to support Ged Baldwin's proposal that at each session of Parliament twenty bills or motions by private Members be selected by draw and brought forward for debate with the assurance that they would be voted on. Thus the Member's idea might still go down in a blaze of attention but not ignominiously. In the words of Conservative backbenchers who parody John Diefenbaker, "Parliament would live!"

Baldwin's idea had a lot of substance. "Most government bills are dredged up from the bowels of the civil service," he said. "The Members of Parliament are closer to the people and should be able to put in bills with the knowledge that they will at least be voted on. Private Members have a great deal more to offer than the public thinks and they should be given the chance. I say this after fifteen years here."

His approach struck a resonant chord within me because even after only thirteen months I could see how the vitality and importance of Parliament were being eroded. There are so many dynamics in our society of escalating change that Parliament is no longer the sole national political force. Big business, big unions, big protest movements, big federal-provincial conferences—these are political forces that the government has to pay attention to. A lot more attention than to Members of Parliament—except when we vote on critical matters, which is infrequent. Baldwin's idea seemed a plausible way to strengthen the input of individual Members. In any event it had now been fed into the machinery.

I looked at my watch. 12:40 p.m. I still had not seen the day's mail or read the briefing document the Party's research office puts out every morning. Back in the office there were three calls from Edmonton waiting to be returned. A pension case. An invitation to speak at a service club. An irate woman protesting that her community group did not receive a LIP grant.

As I was hanging up after this call I opened the research document and there on the first page was an in-depth study of LIP allocations. In eight out of ten provinces constituencies held by Liberals received much more in grants than constituencies held by opposition M.P.s. Why hadn't I read that document before the last phone call, I mumbled to myself.

My junior secretary brought me a sandwich and at the same time announced that she had a job offer in a minister's office that would pay her more money. Since Members cannot control the salaries of their staff, there wasn't much I could do except wish her good luck. I called in my first secretary and told her to start the replacement process. Good second secretaries are hard to find and if the work flow is not kept moving, an office can be in chaos in no time.

Just as I was settling down to read the previous day's Hansard the 2 p.m. House bell started ringing. Ahead of me on the Centre Block stairs were Mr. Diefenbaker, in a grey tweed suit and carrying a brown leather folder, and his protégé Sean O'Sullivan, the youngest Member of Parliament, still in his early twenties. The Opposition lobby was filling up and I stopped to chat for a moment with Walter Dinsdale, one of the senior Members with whom I had become friendly through our mutual interest in handicapped people.

The Speaker was winding up the opening prayers as I stepped through the curtains. Mr. Stanfield sat down, seemingly oblivious to his surroundings, and started signing mail. Warren Allmand, the Solicitor General, walked across the floor to talk to Erik Nielsen who seems to know more about what's going on in all the back rooms than anyone else. The Prime Minister approached his seat wearing rust trousers, a light sport jacket, wool tie and red rose. Stanley Knowles, having finished a discussion with Alistair Fraser, the dignified and deferential Clerk of the House, stopped at Mr. Trudeau's desk. John Turner, ebullient as usual in his banker's grey suit and red tie, set out his daily briefing cards, ready to respond to any question with this latest statistic or that new report.

It was cold in the House. The thermostat had been turned down as some sort of example to the nation of energy conservation. I was never able to learn if the public was impressed with the hardy souls representing them in the Commons. All I knew was that whereas

I had to put on a sweater to go into the Commons, my own office upstairs was so hot I had to keep the window open.

Across from me I noticed Madame Sauvé, Minister of Science and Technology, wearing a coat. I was glad to see her because I had a question ready for her on extending a study of nuclear energy across the country to include the expertise available at the universities of Alberta and British Columbia. The question had been prompted by a University of Alberta professor who felt that the study was based too exclusively in central Canada. I felt that he had a point and sent Madame Sauvé notice that I would ask the question, in the hope that her response would be a substantial one.

The Speaker called for order and Mitchell Sharp was on his feet with a statement designed to glue leaks of government information. Another day's business was underway.

Motions, government bills, private bills, oral questions. Once more the energy issue dominated the Question Period. Mr. Stanfield led off. David Lewis was next. The jeering and catcalls were building up and I could see the Speaker sitting on the edge of his chair. Réal Caouette was protesting the bad manners of Members. Mr. Diefenbaker, his long arm and finger pointed menacingly across the chamber, was chastising the Prime Minister. Half the Question Period was gone and Members in the back rows started standing at each opening in an effort to be recognized. I joined them. Three, five, seven times I was on my feet. I lost count. Suddenly Madame Sauvé, the object of my attention today, picked up her papers and left. The Speaker selected a member near me. He looked at me but in my confusion I couldn't think of another question (though I had about ten in a file upstairs) and stayed seated. The Speaker's eye went right by me.

A minute or so later he called Orders of the Day, the program of legislation to be dealt with, and debate on one of the energy bills resumed. There was so much noise as most Members got up to leave that the Member who had the floor had to wait for a minute for the exodus to finish. Outside I headed for the reading room to check the day's newspapers, a timesaver that enables me to skim four or five papers from different cities in about five minutes. Any article I am really interested in I have photocopied and sent to my office. When I entered my office upstairs it was 3:30 p.m. and John Rolphe, one of Mr. Stanfield's policy aides, was on the phone. "Can you bring me up to date on your decentralization study?" he asked. Stevens had apparently poured a little oil into the machinery since this morning. I arranged to send Rolphe the background information and said I was ready to pursue the subject along any lines Mr. Stanfield wanted.

An officer from the Privy Council had an appointment with me to discuss government information and the public dissemination thereof. He had called a few days earlier and obviously wanted to talk to me, though as we began our conversation I couldn't figure out why. Maybe because of my own communications background, maybe he was doing a random sampling of new Members. I told him about a household mailing I had done to every home in Edmonton-Strathcona outlining good government publications on such subjects as health services, information on drug abuse, consumer protection, housing programs, immigration. I had received three thousand letters asking for publications—a workload that had tied up my secretaries for six weeks. So there's obviously a public need for well-presented information, I said, trying to be as non-partisan as possible as I went on to make the additional point that the government should not treat information vehicles as political propaganda campaigns.

By now it was five o'clock. My secretary was waiting to give me a rundown on correspondence she had handled throughout the day, new cases and more phone calls from Edmonton. I was due at six o'clock at a committee dinner Heath Macquarrie had lined up with Reuben Baetz, executive director of the Canadian Council on Social Development. As chairman of the Progressive Conservative Committee on Health, Welfare and Social Affairs, Macquarrie wanted to get Baetz's ideas as preparation for a policy paper. At 5:30 p.m. Macquarrie's office called to ask if I would come over early to have a pre-dinner drink with Baetz.

I had been following Baetz for several years because of his forceful stands on social advancement and I was anxious to meet him. We chatted briefly with Macquarrie, then walked through the tunnel

linking the West Block to the Centre Block, rode the elevator to the
sixth floor and headed for the New Zealand room, a private dining
room at the rear of the parliamentary restaurant with a panoramic
view of the Ottawa River. I'm always slightly amused when I go
into the parliamentary restaurant because it serves as a focal point
for public criticism of M.P.s who, it is alleged by the occasional reporter on a dull news day, are ripping off the public because our $2
dinners are subsidized. I guess $2 dinners are something everyone
understands. But if the public ever grasped the full extent of the
overruns, duplication and mismanagement contained within the
1973-74 $26 billion federal budget, there would be a revolution on
Parliament Hill.

Baetz lit a cigar as he began to talk about the implications of the
Economic Council of Canada's warning that transfer payments for
social programs—tax money which Ottawa redistributes to promote
social equity—were growing faster than the economy itself. He was
afraid of an indiscriminating public backlash against expenditures
for social programs: "We're disappointed that by engaging in vague
generalizations and failing to distinguish between transfer payments
designed exclusively for the poor and those designed to benefit
eligible Canadians of all income levels, the Economic Council has
made the poor the scapegoat of our inflationary problems. The
Council's latest review leads us to conclude that our social policies
are once again being developed through economic models," he said.

We began to talk about family allowances and Baetz outlined his
conviction that low-income families would benefit more from a radical change in income tax laws rather than the bandaid approach of
increasing family allowances. I would have liked to continue our discussion but most Members present had to go to eight o'clock committee meetings and our session broke up.

I went down to the House. Energy was still being debated. In any
debate the first round of speeches is usually interesting. When a
government piece of legislation is introduced for second reading the
minister responsible gives a lengthy speech, usually forty or fifty
minutes and the spokesman for each party responds by giving his
party's position. The verbosity of the speeches is usually tolerable

on the first round while the subject is fresh. Thereafter, speakers seldom break new ground but put their views on the record either to support their party, demonstrate their familiarity with the subject, or impress the folks back home (I have made speeches for all three reasons). This is not to say that all speeches are therefore dull. Some are exceptional pieces of oratory; some are hilarious. You seldom know in advance when you will get a good one. But the forty-minute time limit, even the twenty-minute rule when it is in effect, results generally in a run of dull speeches.

M.P.s do not feel guilty about leaving the House because committee meetings are scheduled while the House is sitting and the commitment to attend your committee meeting is usually stronger than to sit in Parliament. There is always constituency work waiting to be done. And a reading of Hansard will give you in a few minutes the information obtained in listening to a whole day's expostulations. Nevertheless, it is disconcerting to make a great speech in a near-empty House (being human, most Members consider their own speeches to be great), then step into the lobby and find it crowded with Members watching a hockey game on T.V.

As I sat in my seat in the fifth row under the clock, contemplating what it costs to keep Parliament going and surveying the magnificent chamber, characterized at this moment by a drone in the air, I thought once more of the two things I would institute if I were in command: ten-minute speeches and television.

Constant television coverage would improve the calibre of debating. And with a ten-minute rule a speaker would have to marshal his arguments for effective presentation. Why could not a network of educational T.V. channels be reserved to bring Parliament into homes and classrooms across the country? Public education demands the presence of T.V. in the chamber and if we had it there would be a better spirit of parliamentary cooperation and performance. I had actually fed both these ideas into the machinery via the Procedure and Organization Committee; many Members, I found, had preceded me and the Committee had previously studied, and recommended, T.V. in the House. But as a new Member learns, there's many a step between a recommendation by a House Committee or Royal Commission and its implementation.

By nine o'clock I felt I could spend time more profitably at my desk. I put in some calls to Edmonton (a good time to call since, with the time difference, I was catching people at 7 p.m. before they went out). Usually I try to call the twenty or thirty people closest to me in my political organization at least once every two or three weeks. These are the people who worked hard to put me in Parliament and they appreciate a phone call from Ottawa. For my part I like to chat with them and pick up local news and opinions. These conversations are not meant to be profound analyses of events, though often they prompt a lot of horse-sense reaction from my friends. Rather they keep me close to the group around me and prevent me from sliding off into my own dream world, which would be my natural inclination and certainly the trap for those who begin to think that Parliament Hill is the world.

It was starting to get late so I made a quick dive into the correspondence file, dictating answers to non-routine letters, usually those asking for my opinion or giving me theirs. My secretary had clipped two together, indicating that I should read them consecutively. I smiled as I did so. The first was a copy of a letter a constituent had sent to the local paper: "I recently had problems concerning passport and citizenship papers, and a phone call to Mr. Roche's twenty-four-hour telephone service was promptly returned, but due to my not being home two more calls were made before reaching me—the third call from Ottawa on Sunday. Doug Roche was most sympathetic and gracious regarding my problem and the next morning I was telephoned from here in the city to be informed my problem was rectified. I deeply respect Mr. Roche's interest in my problem and thank him sincerely. I find him a very dedicated, hard-working man, who in my humble opinion is trying valiantly to live up to all the promises made to his constituents."

The other letter struck a different note: "I voted for you but now I'm sorry I did so. Our day care group applied for a LIP grant and we are a far better community service than some outfits that got grants. Why didn't we get a grant? And why didn't you fight to get us one? I'll remember your lack of concern about the 'little people' next election."

That's politics. Some people love you; others hate you. The object is to have the former outnumber the latter. Not just for political survival for its own sake, but survival so you can do what you want to do. There's the crunch. By now it was 10:40 p.m. and there was no more time for musing, or the rest of the file. By leaving now I could walk comfortably to my apartment, enjoying the first air I would have since morning, change into my pyjamas, get a 7-Up and two donuts from the fridge and sit down precisely as the national news was starting on T.V. Kind of a ritual, I suppose, but by letting the 10:40 deadline go by I would dawdle, get home late, and be that much more tired the following day. Besides, tomorrow I had to be up at seven to start the 2,000-mile, seven-hour door-to-door weekly trip back to Edmonton.

I sometimes use a one-line joke for speeches in Edmonton: "People ask me what I like best about Ottawa. What I like best is getting off the plane in Edmonton." Besides being good for a laugh, the line is a perfect reflection of how I feel. I do not want to live in Ottawa, arduous as the travel back and forth is. I don't expect to be in politics the rest of my life and I don't want to cut myself off from my life in Edmonton. The experience of this life so far has indicated to my wife and me that we should stick to our decision not to uproot the family from their life and friendships in Edmonton. In the course of a year there are about sixteen weeks that Parliament does not sit—and I would not want to sit around Ottawa during that time. So I put up with the Monday and Friday flights. The apartment that Evita our eldest daughter and I shared was working out well.

I grabbed my briefcase, stuffed it with correspondence, Hansards, reports to be read and left, already a couple of minutes past my deadline. Evita greeted me on her way to bed and I sank into my chair. When the news was over I felt the need to just sit there and relax so that when I went to bed I would sleep. I put some Judy Garland records on the stereo and though I like Judy full blast, I kept the volume low.

❴ 4 ❵

ON A GOOD DAY

Now it is two years later. December 4, 1975. I'm in my fourth year as a Member of Parliament. A second election has gone by. The election we were supposed to win. But a funny thing happened on our way to victory. Wage-and-price controls. The Conservatives were in favour; the Liberals were not. The voters were definitely opposed and kept Mr. Trudeau in the Prime Minister's office. Now we had both Trudeau and wage-and-price controls. Stanfield was on his way out. What a political lesson.

I remember the night of the election, July 8, 1974. I had arranged that my new secretary in Ottawa, Pamela Miles, would go into my office, turn on the radio at 8 p.m. and phone me in Edmonton to let me hear the early returns from the East. It was only 6 p.m. in Edmonton and since the polls were still open local broadcasts of election results were prohibited. I was just coming out of the shower when the phone rang.

"You aren't going to believe this," Pam said, "but the Liberals are winning a majority."

"You've got it wrong," I said as I sat on the edge of my bed. "It's the Conservatives who are getting a majority."

Instead of arguing with me Pam turned the radio louder. The CBC voice sounded authoritative. Newfoundland was a disaster. Tom Bell was defeated in New Brunswick. Stanfield's own majority was cut. We were being massacred in Toronto. My good friend Terry O'Connor was gone in Halton.

I got dressed slowly and thought about how I should conduct

43

myself in the hours ahead. I would hold my own seat; the deep Conservative strength in Alberta would overcome resistance to wage-and-price controls. But it would be a hollow victory. The cheers would be flat. All my supporters would naturally be depressed at the thought that Trudeau would still be running the country for another four years. I would have to rise above the depression and keep pointing to the future.

I staged the entrance to my campaign headquarters with Eva and the children for 7:58 p.m. The applause came, as I knew it would, but there was a what-are-we-going-to-do-now look on the faces around me. The polls started reporting in. After ten minutes I knew that I was doing even better than in 1972. This time my Liberal opponent was Ches Tanner, an Edmonton alderman and businessman. I liked Tanner but never took him seriously as an opponent. His singing sisters were a great act but Tanner failed to use effectively his best argument: that he should be elected because Alberta desperately needs representation in the federal cabinet. The N.D.P. ran Lila Fahlman, aggressive and emotional, who seemed to get madder at me as the campaign went on largely because I wouldn't fight with her. Lila was clearly throwing away the N.D.P. vote and I kept thinking that the Party would have been smarter to run Howard Leeson again. The Social Credit had Leif Oddson, a courteous and affable businessman, but the Socreds are out in Alberta today. The Communist Party and the Marxist-Leninist spin-off led a pair of candidates that we had to put up with at the forums in the name of democracy.

I still had my essential team around me: Darryl Smith managing the campaign, Shona Wehm coordinating it, Bob Lloyd raising money—we only needed $18,000 this time—Woody Johnson controlling it, Gerry Lock organizing polls, Elaine Paproski running coffee parties, Joe Milner picking up all the pieces and Frank McMillan never far away. I knew the campaign was running badly, chiefly because not enough people really cared about the election. But I didn't want to sound alarmist because victory appeared certain. So we lumbered through the eight weeks and when it was over I had 54.7 per cent of the votes, 5.3 per cent more than in 1972. My majority had increased from 10,283 in 1972 to 11,471 in 1974. As I foresaw, Lila came in with half of Leeson's vote and the transferred N.D.P. vote went mostly to Tanner.

I studied Jack Kennedy's face as he watched my results being posted and listened to the national returns at the same time. Kennedy is an Edmonton lawyer, a leading Conservative in the province and treasurer of the Edmonton-Strathcona P.C. Association. All the years of working for the Conservatives. And always the wilderness. Sure, local victory. But what good is it when the national goes sour? Quebec and the Liberals. How can we ever win when the odds are stacked against us? It was all there on Kennedy's face. After a few moments he quietly left. I didn't blame him.

"Come on," I said to Darryl. "Let's go to the T.V. stations and get these goddamned interviews over with."

I went to the Seattle World's Fair with the family for a post-election vacation, accepted the reality of Stanfield's announcement that he would be stepping down and then went off to Bucharest for the U.N. World Population Conference.

Since my parliamentary life was starting to focus more intensively on the growing problem of mass poverty in the developing world, I was determined to study the population question at the two-week conference, one of a series the U.N. has been holding on global problems. I had applied to the government for status as a parliamentary observer, but somebody, somewhere had decided that no M.P.s would be sent. The P.C. national office was overwhelmed with the debt from the election and wouldn't spend a cent on anything not vital. So I got myself accredited to the conference as a journalist, wrote articles for religious papers in Canada and lined up a lecture series when I returned to pay for the trip. This turned out to be a sound move because it led to an invitation to write a short book, *Justice Not Charity: A New Global Ethic for Canada*, which in turn forced me to study all the reasons why the United Nations is right in calling for a new economic order.

When I returned from the World Population Conference in Bucharest I wrote a feature article for the Toronto *Globe and Mail* in which I quoted a Third World delegate who had described Canada as "a fat cat in a suffering world." The quote summed up, in my view, Canada's attitude to a world undergoing startling change. The newspaper put the quote in the headline, thus drawing a lot of attention to the article. I had previously given weighty speeches (I thought) in Parliament about Canada's role in a changing world—with very little reaction. Since becoming a Member of Parliament I have seldom said or written anything worthwhile that I had not previously said on the floor of the House of Commons and which was duly recorded for posterity in Hansard. Yet with this article I put across more ideas on Canada and the population question than I had ever done in the Commons. A senior cabinet minister stopped me in the hall to say how impressed he was with my criticism of the way technical-minded civil servants had dominated Canada's role in Bucharest. I went to a meeting with some of my colleagues who were discussing our international image and I could tell from their reaction that they were hearing my ideas for the first time—when in fact they had been in a speech given in the House a week earlier.

All of this made me realize—once again—the necessity of an M.P. using all the avenues of communication open to him because he is an M.P. Speeches in an all but deserted House will not do the job. So I ploughed on with my writing and my parliamentary concentration on Canada's role in international development. I was now active on the External Affairs and National Defence Committee. Studying the operation of the Canadian International Development Agency (CIDA) convinced me that a thorough parliamentary examination of Canada's role in international development was necessary and I pressed for the creation of a subcommittee to carry out such a study. After some time the government agreed to issue a House order that would establish a subcommittee with instructions to conduct an in-depth study.

I spent the summer working on *Justice Not Charity*, then went with half a dozen M.P.s to the Seventh Special Session of the United Nations General Assembly in September, 1975, which reaffirmed the principles of a new economic order.

Parliament resumed and again I found myself rushing from meeting to meeting, flying back and forth from Ottawa to Edmonton nearly every weekend, trying to tell myself not to get so over-committed but without much success. I had long since recognized my love-hate feeling about being an M.P.

❧

On good days feelings of accomplishment flowed through me like blood rushing through my body. Small accomplishments perhaps but they made me feel alive. December 4 was a good day.

I awoke in my Ottawa apartment at 7:30 a.m. The morning news highlighted the plight of a trainload of hostages on a hijacked train in Holland. The closet door in my bedroom pulled off its hinges, convincing me that the Club of Rome was right in stating that people care about their problems at hand, not about those in another part of the world. Evita, now a second-year law student at the University of Ottawa, was brimming over with happiness at the results of an exam and the presentation she had made to her class on the constitutional aspects of wage-and-price controls.

I could see the Gatineau Hills as we sat in the living room chatting —something we didn't do often enough. The day was clear and brisk as I stepped into a taxi at 8:40, heading for the Lester B. Pearson Building, headquarters of the External Affairs Department.

I had arranged an appointment with J. G. Hadwen, an External Affairs senior officer, for four Romanian men who were trying to have their wives and children released from Romania. The four men David Pompiliu of Toronto, Dimitrie Moldovan of Edmonton, Julian Hirtescu of Toronto and Alexandre Sandu of Quebec City had been standing outside the Parliament Buildings for a week with signs urging Canada to intercede with Romania for reunification of families. The first few days I saw the men I didn't pay much attention. Protesters are a common sight on Parliament Hill. But the calm demeanor and polite greeting from these men each morning finally got through to me and on December 2 I stopped to talk to them. They told me that they had escaped from Romania more than two years ago, were now settled as landed immigrants in Canada and needed help to get their families released. By coincidence External Affairs Minister Allan MacEachen was tabling that day in the House a document entitled "The Final Act of the Conference on Security and Cooperation in Europe" and I had been asked to reply to his speech on behalf of our Party. The document, bearing the signatures of thirty-five nations which had come together at Helsinki, is a very controversial one because it gives the appearance of legitimizing the political boundaries of the east European countries dominated by Russia after World War II. I am critical of the Act because it virtually recognizes Soviet control over eastern Europe. But it does have several good sections, one of them being on the reunification of families. The Act states that "participating states will deal in a positive and humanitarian spirit with the applications of persons who wish to be reunited with members of their families."

Why not bring the four men into the gallery as my guests so that I could point to them while making my speech urging action by the Canadian government in helping them? The idea seemed sensible enough, even though the Speaker wouldn't like my singling out people in the gallery. I told the men they would have to wear ties and jackets. They went to their hotel to change and I brought them into the House. "How can we expect people to believe in the Helsinki Final Act if we do not see very quick action in the reunification of families?" I said in my speech. MacEachen had agreed to study the cases. The Romanians had been jubilant as we went off to the cafeteria and interviews with the press.

The appointment with Hadwen was for 9 a.m. and the men were waiting when I walked into the Pearson Building lobby. Once I had introduced them to Hadwen and his staff officers, there was no real need of my staying because I couldn't help much in the discussion of the technical aspects of the cases. I asked for a follow-up report and went downstairs to the waiting taxi.*

I was due at a committee meeting at 9:30 but stopped in my office first.

"The Chinese Ambassador's secretary called," my secretary said

---

*Consistent pressure over the next few months produced exit visas from Romania for the families involved. On May 21, 1976 the External Affairs Department reported to me that the wife and child of Dimitrie Moldovan of Edmonton would be permitted to leave Romania.

as I hung up my coat. "The Ambassador wants to accept your invitation to dinner." A few days earlier I had written to Ambassador Chang Wen-chin, at his suggestion, requesting permission to visit China to study development in that country.

"Call his secretary back and suggest next Monday night," I told Pam as I picked up my *Time-Reader's Digest* file and rushed for the little green bus that transports M.P.s from building to building on Parliament Hill.

The Parliamentary Committee on Broadcasting, Films and Assistance to the Arts was in the midst of a stormy series of meetings on Bill C-58, the government measure that would end the special privileges enjoyed by *Time* magazine and *Reader's Digest*. I don't normally serve on the Committee but had joined it for examination of this bill because Gordon Fairweather, in charge of the debate for the Conservatives, had asked me to. However much I want to help Canadian publications, I think the government's move against *Time* and *Reader's Digest*, both of which have over a period of many years built up extensive Canadian operations, is unfair. Seeing both sides of the argument and relying on my own journalistic experience, I felt I might be able to help produce an accommodation that would satisfy both the government and the Opposition.

Today Secretary of State Hugh Faulkner was to appear again before the Committee. The hearings had not been going well for the government (though, of course, they had the manpower for the final showdown) and I wanted to question Faulkner one last time to try to find a middle course that would allow *Reader's Digest* and *Time* to continue operating and at the same time give a boost to Canadian publications.

The meeting in room 209 in the West Block had already started when I arrived. Faulkner and his taxation expert from Revenue Canada, J. S. Hodgson, were testifying. I signalled the chairman, Jacques Guilbault, that I wanted to ask questions; with a flick of his eyes to the clock he indicated that time would run out before his list of questioners could be completed.

Rod Blaker, the Liberal Member for Lachine, and Hodgson were locked in a convoluted discussion about ways in which *Reader's*

Digest could do indirectly what Bill C-58 would prohibit directly. Faulkner had determined to have publications in Canada conform to the government's arbitrary decision that, in order to qualify for tax deductions for advertisers, the magazine would have to be eighty per cent different in content from foreign publications. The eighty per cent content rule was the core of the argument as far as I was concerned. I had argued in the House on second reading that publications should be seventy-five per cent Canadian owned and licensed in Canada (if *Time* and *Reader's Digest* wouldn't meet those conditions I would not argue on their behalf, but all the indications were that they would). It would be unfair to apply an eighty per cent content rule and have it measured by bureaucrats who would be given arbitrary power to decide whether a publication was sufficiently different.

As the chairman had predicted, time ran out before I could speak. By a coincidence the next meeting I was scheduled to attend was in this same room.

The Subcommittee on International Development has been my chief interest in Parliament. Very few people even know of its existence, let alone what it does. The press seldom comes near us. We don't fight and roar at one another; rather we are trying together to figure out the most realistic things Canada can do to help the developing nations plug into international systems of trade and commerce and hence become more self-reliant. Not much copy in this—at least not by the standards of journalism that apply today.

I remember when the social irresponsibility of the media was really brought home to me. About a year earlier when the External Affairs Committee was probing the estimates of the Canadian International Development Agency and we were warming to the wider subject of the new economic order, as distinct from just giving aid, Maurice Strong came before the Committee. A former president of CIDA, he was at that time head of the U.N. environment program. He made an eloquent plea for strong Canadian support of the "minimum goal" of world development. "That goal," he said, "is that there would be enough food, shelter, medicine and education for every human being on earth. That is the minimum to protect human dignity and decency. Anything less is declaring bankruptcy in our civilization."

Not a journalist was present to report these words. But an hour after the Strong meeting the Justice Committee opened hearings into charges that politicians were involved in corruption in the dredging industry, centring around work done in Hamilton harbour. The press, radio and T.V. journalists flocked in even before the meeting started. The smell of scandal was in the air and everyone was hungry.

Our witness today was Gerald Helleiner, an economics professor at the University of Toronto and founder of the new North-South Institute which is examining Canada's role in international development. Helleiner had come to the Committee a week earlier but we had only been four minutes into the meeting when the division bells in the House of Commons rang; we had to return for a vote and that was the end of the meeting. Today he was back to discuss with us his reaction to Canada's new Five-Year Strategy for International Development Cooperation which provides for the first time "a comprehensive and organic approach" to relations with developing countries.

The Strategy is too rhetorical, Helleiner said as he warmed to his subject. The Generalized System of Preferences, touted by the government as a key non-aid instrument, is "nothing short of ludicrous" because it exempts textiles and footwear, precisely those products the developing world wants to sell to us. I could see Herb Breau, a Liberal from New Brunswick, wincing a little at this criticism. Textiles are a sore subject with many M.P.s worried about the declining Canadian textile industry. The domestic market is hurt not by the poor countries, however, but by imports from developed countries. A complex subject but Helleiner was moving our study along.

At 1 p.m. I was back in my office where there were requests for two phone interviews right away with radio reporters. One wanted to talk about agriculture, the other about modernizing the post office. I only had time for one, so I chose the post office since I can always fire off a few words about what a terrible service it is, whereas my knowledge of agriculture is thin at the best of times.

I had arranged a 1:30 phone call from Geoffrey Stevens, the *Globe and Mail* political columnist who had been following the *Time-Reader's Digest* affair very closely and was, in fact, writing the most incisive criticism of it of any journalist. We talked about Faulkner's relentless defence of the eighty per cent content rule rather than using anti-dumping legislation. This would protect Canadian publications by imposing higher tariffs on imported material. I knew that tomorrow's column would be a hot one.

I went to the Opposition lobby a few minutes before 2 p.m. because the Conservative Members on the Broadcasting Committee were caucusing. Extra meetings were coming up because of the prolonged opposition battle. But I had firm plans to go to Edmonton that evening. I had long since decided that casual sudden meetings did not deserve a high priority.

The second bell to start the House proceedings sounded and we filtered into the House. Elmer MacKay, the mild-mannered Nova Scotia lawyer who is one of the deadliest critics in the Opposition, was on his feet.

"Mr. Speaker," he said, "I rise on a matter of urging and pressing necessity." This is a daily ploy under Standing Order 43 to bring some matter onto the floor for a momentary spotlight. Very seldom does any action follow from what is proposed since unanimous consent is required. Some issues raised are frivolous, but day by day MacKay had been building a strong case to show that Liberal political patronage made a mockery out of a supposed bidding system for federal concessions—which had been grabbed by Sky Shops. The House was quiet as MacKay put forth his motion "that the Solicitor General, for the benefit and information of Members of Parliament, table forthwith copies of all documents which are now public, including warrants obtained by the R.C.M.P. in regard to the current investigations in respect of Sky Shops, Mirabel, the Olympic Village and related matters."

The motion was denied unanimous consent by government Members, but MacKay had made his point and followed it up in the Question Period: get the key documents into the House where they can be debated, or lay charges and have the courts deal with the matter.

Mr. Stanfield opened the Question Period by asking Finance Minister Donald Macdonald to clarify policy statements by the chairman of the Anti-Inflation Board. This went on for a few exchanges but my mind was concentrating on a question of my own. I kept my eye on the Speaker, looking for an opening.

About twenty-five minutes into the Question Period, the Speaker jumped from the first to the fifth row and it was my turn to speak.

"Mr. Speaker," I said, looking across the aisle at Pierre Trudeau to see if I had his attention, "I have a question for the Prime Minister. In view of the strong protest made at Tuesday night's meeting of the External Affairs Committee concerning the impending sale of a Canadian nuclear reactor to South Korea, and precisely because South Korea has recently purchased a reprocessing plant from France which will give Korea the capacity to build a nuclear device, is the government determined to complete that sale without a further review of the wisdom of this policy, as advocated by many people in Canada, including the distinguished Canadian, General E. L. M. Burns?"

The Prime Minister replied, "With respect, Mr. Speaker, I believe the Secretary of State for External Affairs answered questions along similar lines not more than two days ago."

This was dodging the question so I asked a supplementary: "Precisely because the issue was raised at the External Affairs Committee meeting, I will again put the question to the Prime Minister. With respect to the trustworthiness of South Korea, with whom we will be signing an agreement, has the Prime Minister examined the reports by impartial international observers such as Amnesty International, the International Commission of Jurists, the International League for the Rights of Man and the World Conference of Religion for Peace that are highly critical of the Park regime?"

Mr. Trudeau: "Mr. Speaker, these are the kinds of representations that could usefully be made when the Minister is in attendance before the Committee."

I was incensed. It was precisely because these very representations had been made by me and others in the Committee without any results that I was now raising the issue in the House with the Prime Minister. But what does he say? See the Minister in committee. This little game is a good example of how the rights of Members of Parliament are continually trampled on by a government that cares little for parliamentary approval or disapproval; and the nuclear issue is crucial to planetary survival.

One has to be coldly analytical about the political process and not allow rebuffs to be taken personally. Keep fighting. That's what this game is all about. Jim McGrath, the fiery Newfoundland Conservative, gave a demonstration of this a few minutes later when he jumped to his feet at the end of Question Period to protest Agriculture Minister Whelan's failure to provide replies. McGrath went further, criticizing the provisional rules which do not permit points of order during Question Period so that by the time a Member is permitted—after the Question Period—to protest, the Minister concerned may have left the House, which is precisely what happened to McGrath.

I had to get back to my office, but I was still angry over Trudeau's nonchalant attitude toward the nuclear issue. Ever since India set off a nuclear bomb by reprocessing the spent fuel from a Candu reactor which we had sold them, I had become convinced that Canada should sell no more nuclear reactors until stringent international safeguards are in place. The threat to safety does not lie in the possession of a Candu reactor but rather in the use which is made of the spent fuel from the reactor. By constructing a separation or re-processing plant it is possible to produce plutonium, the stuff from which nuclear bombs can be made. Therefore, the disposition of the spent fuel becomes the all-important question in attempting to impose safeguards against the misuse of the reactor. The reliability of the country to whom we sell a Candu reactor is essential. And I don't think South Korea (or Argentina, for that matter, another Candu purchaser) is reliable.

I am convinced that in this instance money—Candu reactors sell for $500 million—triumphs over morality and safety. There are now 650 nuclear plants in thirty-eight countries; half a dozen countries have the capacity to make nuclear bombs and the technology is spreading quickly. The International Atomic Energy Agency, a U.N. affiliate which admits it doesn't have nearly enough inspectors, reported that in 1975 only ninety-five per cent of the plutonium extracted from the radium waste of reactors could be accounted for with accuracy; the remaining five per cent is enough plutonium to make fifty-five nuclear bombs. In other words the rapid escalation of nuclear reactors is producing more plutonium than can be effectively monitored. Even when the reactors are being used for the peaceful production of energy, the danger of deliberate diversion of plutonium for a nuclear bomb grows. No wonder the scientists themselves are worried.

All this had been on my mind when I questioned Allan MacEachen in the External Affairs Committee two nights earlier. The following extract from the proceedings shows how difficult (if not impossible) it is for an M.P. to turn the government away from a preselected course. MacEachen confirmed at the opening of the meeting that Canada and South Korea would shortly sign a nuclear agreement.

Mr. Roche: Have you, sir, taken into account the repeated representation made by General Burns, the distinguished authority in this field, warning Canada not to enter into an agreement with South Korea because of the instability of the regime?

Mr. MacEachen: Mr. Chairman, when we undertook to deal with South Korea we considered all these factors very, very carefully.

Mr. Roche: Have you, as the Minister, examined the report of Amnesty International, the International Commission of Jurists, the International League for the Rights of Man, and the World Conference of Religion for Peace?

Mr. MacEachen: No, I have not examined these reports in detail.

Mr. Roche: On October 23 in Parliament I made a speech on this subject giving details and it is now December 2, and the Minister says he has not even heard of what I said in the House of Commons. Why do we go into the House of Commons to make speeches, Mr. Minister?

Mr. MacEachen: I listened to you, Mr. Roche, telling me of the factors that were raised by the groups you mentioned. All these factors were considered by the government—the political situation in South Korea, the geopolitical factors surrounding

South Korea, the nature of the government within the country —and I can only apologize that I have not studied your speech but I assure you that I know the relevant factors were considered . . .

Mr. Roche: Yesterday, we had a conference with General Burns, who is far more knowledgeable than myself in this area, and he assured me that he is not satisfied, has not been responded to, and is greatly worried about the impending deal that Canada is going to enter into because of our responsibility to give leadership and the passing off of this as helping developing nations by giving nuclear energy. Where did this idea get started from, and how do we protect the world from the escalation of nuclear bombs under the guise of nuclear energy? That is the issue.

Mr. MacEachen: Well that is an issue, of course it is an issue, and I do not think it is fair to say that we are attempting to, in a sense, spread nuclear technology, or distribute nuclear materials under the guise of development.

Mr. Roche: The Prime Minister said that.

Mr. MacEachen: It is a specific obligation we have undertaken within the international community to share our technology with developing countries; and certainly the Republic of Korea is a developing country. It is, I am happy to state, developing reasonably satisfactorily. It has very slight indigenous power resources. It has been badly hurt by the quadrupling in the price of imported oil; which it depends on for its development. The Republic of Korea looks to nuclear energy as an important source. That is a real question.

We have undertaken to provide them with a reactor. We have done so only after negotiating with them a very comprehensive nuclear safeguards agreement, and only after the Republic of Korea has undertaken to become a signatory to the Nonproliferation Treaty. As I have stated, under that treaty it has agreed to put its total nuclear capacity under international safeguards . . .

As the meeting wore on and other Opposition M.P.s carried on the attack, I noticed the Chairman, Maurice Dupras, consulting with the Liberal Whip. Dupras knew a vote was coming on the item covering nuclear energy and so he simply made sure the Liberal Whip kept the Liberal side of the table staffed with more M.P.s than the Opposition. This is an easy procedure since the rules permit any M.P. to be appointed to a committee—if there is room—on a moment's notice. Thus time after time Opposition M.P.s are confronted with the spectacle of new government M.P.s arriving at the last minute to fill up their roster and vote with the government—without the slightest idea of what is being discussed. No matter how good a case may have been presented by the Opposition, their motions will not be accepted—if the government Whip is doing his job. Of course, it works both ways. Opposition M.P.s are sometimes rushed into a committee to vote with their colleagues. The point is that in a majority government there is no way a committee vote can go against the government unless government M.P.s assert their independence of the Whip.

I tried to make the point while MacEachen was still present that we would vote against the nuclear energy appropriation, as a symbolic protest, because the terms of the South Korea Candu deal were being kept secret from us. Although I wanted to read my protest in MacEachen's presence to try to get a further reaction from him, Dupras would not let me. After MacEachen and his entourage of officials had left, we called for a recorded vote and lost eleven to eight. I looked into the faces of some Liberal M.P.s who had just joined the Committee and saw nothing but the bland expression of men doing their routine job.

On the way back to my office after Question Period I kept trying to think of something more that might be done to block the Candu sale to South Korea. Stanfield himself had demanded a moratorium on sales months ago. The government didn't listen to him. They probably wouldn't start listening to me.*

*On January 30, 1976, MacEachen announced in the House that Canada had signed agreements to sell reactors to South Korea and Argentina. He provided background papers on nuclear safeguards and pointed out that Korea had cancelled its order for a reprocessing plant from France; under questioning he conceded that if South Korea changed its mind and acquired a reprocessing plant, the agreement with Canada would not be automatically suspended. On May 18 MacEachen informed the House that Canada would end nuclear co-operation with India (it had been suspended following the detonation of a nuclear device in 1974) because India would not agree to refrain from more nuclear explosions, even for peaceful purposes.

Jack Shea, the parliamentary liaison officer of the Canadian International Development Agency, was in my office to go over details of a CIDA consultation the next week in Ste. Marguerite, Quebec. Development experts from around the world were being brought in to give their reaction to Canada's aid program. I was one of four M.P.s invited. There was only a minute to talk to Shea because I had to get back to the Broadcasting Committee where I would have my chance to question Hugh Faulkner.

"Pam," I said to my secretary, "get the file on all the material on the leadership candidates ready. I'll take it to Ste. Marguerite and read it there." I didn't give any more thought to the decision awaiting me in that file.

At 3:40 p.m. I was back in the West Block committee room in time for this banter which opened the meeting:

> *The Chairman:* Order, gentlemen. We will now resume consideration of Bill C-58, an Act to Amend the Income Tax Act.
> May I have some order, please? Thank you very much.
> Before going forward with the meeting, I guess we have to know what we are talking about.
> *Mr. Friesen:* That never stopped us before.
> *Mr. Fairweather:* What a novel suggestion.
> *An Hon. Member:* You are going to create a bad precedent.

The Chairman tried to get us back on the track by presenting the latest report of an organizational committee which had decided to start a clause-by-clause study of the bill at extra meetings tonight and Friday; questioning of the Minister at this afternoon's meeting would be restricted to five minutes per Member.

I decided that all I would be able to accomplish in five minutes would be a final appeal for fairness. I argued that the government had been unfair to *Time Canada* and *Reader's Digest* in previously indicating that a fifty per cent different content formula would be acceptable and then jumping the figure to eighty per cent, leaving both publications only six weeks to comply. Actually I am opposed to any content rule for a publication owned and licensed in Canada. I was willing to compromise up to fifty per cent but the eighty per cent rule would destroy the nature of both publications. Faulkner responded that the government had decided to stick to the eighty per cent figure in order to protect the Canadian publishing industry. With the chairman warning me that I had used up my five minutes, I just had time for a final shot that Faulkner was defending "a totally unworkable policy."

A moment later the Minister was gone. No accommodation. No amendments. Goodbye *Time Canada* and the Canadian edition of *Reader's Digest*—or so it seemed.*

I had to start thinking about my flight home. The flight was leaving at 6 p.m. which meant I should be in a taxi by 5 p.m. It was past 4:30 and I had to get back to my office in the Centre Block. I headed for the tunnel and at 4:45 I burst into my office with fifteen minutes to sign mail (much of it composed by my secretary and that I would be seeing for the first time), return phone calls, collect papers and reading material for the flight.

Bernie Wood of the Parliamentary Centre for Foreign Affairs and Trade stopped in to talk about research material I would need for an inter-parliamentary conference in Mexico in April. Trying not to be rude I suggested Mexico could wait awhile.

Paul Jackson, the parliamentary correspondent for the Edmonton and Calgary newspapers, was on the phone to get some of my comments on the South Korea nuclear issue. He was writing a story right away so I had to use up the last available minutes on this subject. (When it appeared in the Edmonton *Journal* the headline read: "Roche's Anti-nuclear Crusade Fails".)

I looked at my watch: 5:10 p.m. Pam had my papers and ticket ready.

"Have a great weekend," I said, half-running to the elevator.

---

*Over the Christmas recess the government gave in to the intense pressure mounted by Liberal M.P.s in Quebec to save *Reader's Digest*, which creates many jobs in Quebec as well as printing a French-Canadian edition. The government simply ruled that the digest nature of the publication would enable it to qualify under the new law. Bill C-58 was passed on that basis and *Time Canada* shut down. The Senate did not like Bill C-58 and tried unsuccessfully to change its provisions so that a court, not a bureaucrat, would determine if a publication qualified under the eighty per cent rule.

"I called a Diamond Cab," she said.

Downstairs at the front door no cab was in sight. "Damn it, he's left because I'm late," I muttered to myself. 5:20 p.m. Leave now or forget about the flight. I spotted a Blue Line Cab coming up the hill and moved out to intercept him. I opened the door and the driver looked at me.

"Are you Mr. ——?"

"Yeah," I cut him off. "Listen can you make the airport in twenty-five minutes?"

He groaned but said he'd try.

I slumped into the back seat, feeling a twinge of guilt at having "stolen" the cab but a much more powerful feeling of happiness that I was on my way home.

At 5:45 we were at the airport. I gave the driver a tip, bought some newspapers and asked the stewardess to bring me a drink as soon as we took off.

In the air I started thinking "Edmonton." Living and working in two different locations two thousand miles apart produces a sort of schizophrenic effect. It's two different kinds of existences. Different people. Different problems. Different wardrobes. Different lifestyles. People, especially constituents, seem to depend on me more in Edmonton than they do in Ottawa. This makes me respond better and I always have the feeling that I'm a better M.P. when I'm in Edmonton than when I'm in Ottawa. It's worn out by now but I still use the one-liner about getting off the plane in Edmonton.

At the moment, however, I was getting off the plane in Toronto to make the connection for Edmonton. I headed for CP's first class lounge and phoned Betty Mitchell, my constituency office secretary in Edmonton, who looks after all the cases constituents bring to me in an organized way that I could never manage. She's been deeply interested in politics for many years and has excellent political judgment, which is one reason she was elected a delegate from Edmonton-Strathcona to the forthcoming leadership convention. After we finished discussing the next day's schedule I said, "By the way, Betty, would you remind Eva of the reception that Joe Clark is holding tonight in Edmonton. I'd like her to represent me and she's really interested in Joe's candidacy. Tell Joe I'm in the air and I'm sorry I can't make it."

At 7:30 I settled into the second plane for the three-and-a-half hour trip from Toronto to Edmonton and started looking forward to dinner. I hadn't eaten since breakfast (when you look forward to an airplane dinner, you're really hungry). I hoped no one on the plane would recognize me and come up to talk. I know this makes me sound like a prima donna but I have been saddled countless times with Alberta people I don't know but who recognize me and decide to give me their company for a couple of hours because they have nothing to do and think that I am just dying for conversation. Actually on most plane trips—and tonight was certainly a case— what I want is some peace so that I can read or think or sleep but most of all just be by myself. By the time I get on a plane I'm worn out and not interested in either chit-chat or another harangue about what's wrong with the government. So I've learned to protect myself by putting my nose into a book or a file or papers and grunting in monosyllables if anyone should speak to me. I'm well aware that this anti-social behaviour does not make life easier for my campaign manager but I take the view that my survival comes first and I need a lot of time to myself.

Tonight instead of a book I started going through the newspapers I had accumulated through the day but hadn't yet read. The New York *Times* reported that the Soviet grain crop would be one-third less than expected. This would spell disaster for Russia and provide tempting markets for Canadian exporters—at the very time the developing world ought to claim a priority on our grain exports. I tore out an interesting story on how China is mechanizing its farms for my China file. In the second section I saw a tiny story, almost a filler, noting that Canada's House of Commons had given final approval to the government's wage-and-price control legislation. (Well, I didn't; I voted against it because I feel that the three-year program is too long and too selective to cure inflation and also keep production high.) It never ceases to amaze me how under-reported Canada is in the U.S. press whereas our communications media (Bill C-58 notwithstanding) are filled with U.S. news, politics and entertainment.

The *Globe and Mail* had a letter from somebody complaining that M.P.s' pensions are too generous. Not by my standards they aren't! O.K., so I'm biased. But the great national debates we have over M.P.s' salaries, pensions and meals in the parliamentary restaurant are short-sighted and not helpful to the democratic process. I don't mean that politicians should be able to write their own ticket without any accountability. But the preoccupation of the media with the salary question has created in the public the impression that we are plunderers. Our salaries ($24,000 plus a tax-free expense allowance of $10,600) are not high when related to the expenses of our life. My business friends in Edmonton who are members of my own political organization all make more money than I do.

From a monetary point of view I am not any better off today, and my standard of living has not increased, than when I was editor of the *Western Catholic Reporter*. My wife has her own professional career which is the main reason—I tell myself—that she works; nonetheless we need her income. The expenses of our children, in their teen and college years, are high.

This is beginning to sound like a giant complaint. It's not. We're not starving. We took the family to Jasper for five days at Christmas. The point is that if I really wanted to make some money I would get out of politics. That's why I get irritated when I see criticism repeatedly hurled at us. When Gordon Fairweather opened his personal finances to the scrutiny of a journalist who subsequently reported that Fairweather was in debt, a relative of mine was shocked. "How can it be that a distinguished parliamentarian like Gordon Fairweather who has given his life to Canada isn't paid enough to keep him out of debt?" he asked. "We ought to be ashamed of ourselves for doing this to him."

As far as pensions are concerned, we should be eligible for them after six years' service precisely because of the high risk factor in losing our jobs. There ought to be a minimum age for eligibility and that would be a needed improvement. But considering the demands of the job, the goldfish-bowl existence and so much separation from the family, the pension formula ($4,836 per year after six years' service) is not overly generous.

No issue in the opening months of the Thirtieth Parliament attracted as much attention as the government move to increase our salaries fifty per cent (later reduced to thirty-three per cent). The public fury disturbed M.P.s. The scorn of the media, the indignation of letter-writers, not to mention abusive telephone calls, was like a tidal wave breaking over a reef. On the surface the raise was too high but spread over several years it was less than the composite wage settlement index. But it was perceived as inflationary at a time when Canadians were being asked to tighten their belts.

As the issue mounted in intensity it transcended the "grasping wretches," as one editorialist designated us. I became convinced that people were protesting not only salary increases but the failure of the government and Members of Parliament to run society the way people want.

The public has been unnerved by continuing double-digit inflation, high food prices (not to mention rotten eggs and slaughtered calves), the energy war between Ottawa and the producing provinces and the murders of policemen. On top of all this global conditions are even more unsettling: massive famine, over-population, energy shortage, the arms race, monetary chaos. In the face of so much confusion and a seeming lack of bold solutions, the pay-raise issue gave vent to a backlash. "What right do M.P.s have to raise their salaries when they can't even run the country?" was the charge really being made.

I received more mail and phone calls on this subject than any other except capital punishment and abortion. This letter from one of my constituents, Stanley G. Deane, reflects the intensity and depth of the comments I received:

> I wish to protest most vigorously the action of the government in proposing to grant a fifty per cent increase in parliamentary salaries, and to further increase tax free grants to Members.
> In terms of the present inflation with which Canadians are trying to cope, and particularly in view of the government's

appeals for restraints in salary demands, the present proposals are a most blatant example of hypocrisy and cynicism. When one views the niggardly increases the government offers pensioners and certain classes of civil servants, the increases proposed for parliamentarians become an insult to the intelligence of the electorate, and an indication of the degree of credence given to the ordinary Canadian on Parliament Hill. . . .

This letter succinctly reveals the temper of Canadians today. Of course there is public resentment against M.P.s protecting ourselves against inflation by merely voting the problem away. But the deeper antipathy is caused by the public perception that we are unable to come to grips with the problems that cause people to think society is out of control. This raises the fundamental question of who is making the key decisions affecting Canadian life and what are the criteria for these decisions.

Obviously if parliamentarians are seen to be just another organized group trying to wrest advantage from society by arbitrary action, Parliament will lose whatever moral justification it may have to make decisions binding on others. If it loses its power of moral suasion, what will it use to back up its legal powers? The results are not difficult to predict: individuals and groups will seek to preserve what they have even at the expense of the general welfare. In Canada the structure of our society virtually assures the emergence of ethnic, class and sectional conflict if no single, national and respected body speaks for its citizens as a whole. The credibility of Parliament in a world of frightening and escalating change is then a prime issue. The pay raise issue further damaged a credibility already sinking lower than we like to admit.

Dinner had come and gone. We were coming up over Winnipeg. The night was clear at 35,000 feet and moonlight reflected off the clouds below. I had been dozing but now I was awake again.

I suddenly realized that I had not phoned Isobel Holmes to get the latest report on her husband. Dr. Bob Holmes, a very soft-spoken, thoughtful M.P. from Lambton-Kent in Ontario, had become one of my close friends in Parliament. A short time before he had suffered a severe heart attack. I had talked to Isobel once but wanted to keep in close touch with Bob. Yet the day had gone by without the phone call made. "My God," I muttered to myself, "do I have to be so busy that I can't take the time for my friends?"

I picked up the Toronto *Star* (not my favourite paper but I think this is a subjective reaction conditioned during the days when, as a young Toronto *Telegram* reporter, I had to compete against it in the bizarre newspaper war that enlivened Toronto at that time; I remember racing a team of *Star* reporters across Canada to get to Moose Jaw first and thus pick up photographs of people involved in a Trans-Canada Airlines tragedy before the competition got there). Richard Gwyn's column was headlined "Could Television Revive Parliament?" Although the headline amused me—we've been around this track so many times—I read it with great interest. Nothing more dramatically illustrates the antiquated character of parliamentary rules than the absence of television coverage. Whenever I am in Edmonton I see on my T.V. set during the evening news film clips of the Edmonton city council, the Alberta legislature as well as the United Nations in session. But the business of the Parliament of Canada is conveyed to the public by mob scenes of reporters thrusting microphones into the face of some politician—government or Opposition variety—who has said something spectacular in the House and is now asked to "elaborate" on it. This is not coverage of the House of Commons. It is artificial hokum that the more publicity-conscious M.P.s deliberately exploit by rushing into issues or charges that they know will result in an invitation to go on camera. I am not so much concerned with these personal vanities but I am concerned that the thirty-second clip style of electronic journalism that reporters fall back on because they cannot report the actual Commons events grotesquely distorts what the House really does. It is not the job of journalism to make politicians look any better or worse than they are but to record as objectively as possible significant events. Obviously to do this they must be able to bring their cameras and microphones into the House. None of this is news. In fact it has been debated in committees for so long that the subject has become a joke.

Many M.P.s are now accepting what appears to be a new fact of life in modern Canada: the irrelevancy of Parliament. To begin with, Pierre Trudeau has himself downgraded Parliament. He introduced his wage-and-price control program to the nation via a T.V. speech and never once debated the measure in Parliament. He seldom makes a speech and in all the years Stanfield questioned him on hundreds of subjects his answers were laconic, desultory, uninformative and just plain uncooperative. Apparently the man means it when he says that M.P.s are "nobodies."

The problem, however, is much deeper than the Trudeau personality. The key issues today are not being settled in Parliament. Federal-provincial conferences settle the price of oil and gas as well as apportion the cost of social programs. The federal bureaucracy settles the big spending questions in defence and CIDA matters. A Royal Commission is examining the corporate power of conglomerates. The northern pipeline and native rights issue is in the hands of a judge. A new tri-level process of federal-provincial-municipal consultation is working out the enormous social costs of urbanization. All these devices are useful but ought not to subsume Parliament which is absolutely central to the democratic process. We make the laws. Isn't that relevant? Laws concerning how much tax you will pay, whether capital punishment will prevail, what kind of transportation you will have.

Parliament is supreme. But Gwyn was right when he began his column by discussing the empty seats in the galleries: "The contrast is familiar, and sad. Above, the empty galleries; below, a private club of parliamentarians who shout at each other, and declaim, and posture, because they know that no one—most of the time—is listening. When an institution is dying you don't attack it. It isn't nice. Better to ignore it; safer also, because no one will notice what you've done."

T.V. is not the total answer. But it is a start. The subject has been researched to death. All the evidence is in. The government finally proposed on June 11, 1975 a motion to establish radio and T.V. coverage of Parliament. But on this night six months later, nothing more had been heard of the motion.

It was 10:30 (12:30 in Ottawa) when the taxi deposited me in front of my home. The kids were still awake and we sat around the kitchen counter. Doug had just come in from playing hockey; I never ask him if he's won or lost but I can usually tell. Mary Anne had been at band practice and, although she's pretty cool, I knew she was happy to be playing a short oboe solo at the forthcoming Christmas concert. Patti, who bubbles at everything, was telling us about her misadventures as a basketball referee. In these family enclaves I always tease Eva about "what did you do today?" and usually her exploits teaching at a community college are the most interesting activities of everyone. It had been ten days since I'd seen them and I sat there in real delight at such a terrific family. It was the best moment of the day.

Finally we broke up and Eva and I went upstairs.

"Oh, by the way," she said, "Joe Clark had a very successful reception tonight."

"Good crowd?"

"Very good, and they liked the way he answered questions, firmly and directly."

"That's the way Joe is. He's really establishing himself for the next convention."

"He says he's running for the leadership now, not next time. And also, he told me that after he becomes leader he's going to have you and the other M.P.s out on the road selling the Conservatives one weekend a month."

"Thank you very much," I said, switching off the light. "Right now I'm not interested in travelling anywhere."

⁕{ 5 }⁕

THIS TIME, NOT NEXT TIME

Nothing has taught me so much about politics as my experiences in the Progressive Conservative leadership convention.

A leadership convention is not just a four-day frenzy of speeches and hoopla. That's what the television audience sees. It also consists of battle plans worthy of Clausewitz, the homespun psychology of Joyce Brothers, the histrionics of Jack Lemmon, the endurance of Sir Edmund Hillary. It is months of roadwork with torturous scheduling, meetings that never seem to end, terrible meals at midnight when you discover you haven't eaten all day. A leadership convention is drama, philosophy, spectacle, game and conquest, all of which exist in interior loneliness as well as in the clamour of the arena. I had never been through one before. When it was over I felt that a major turning point in my life had been reached.*

Our convention began in those desolate hours of Stanfield's third defeat in the election of July 8, 1974. Many a Conservative politician went to bed that night knowing Stanfield was finished and wondering . . . maybe . . . what if . . . could I?

A few days later, when my own emotions had settled a bit, I decided to write an article on why Stanfield should be persuaded to

---

*The reader will understand that what follows is not a complete account or even an overview of the leadership convention. It is rather a description of my observations and activities. I am writing of events from my perspective and decisions I made based on what I was able to learn at the time. The chapter must stand within its own framework of time and not be affected by events following the convention.

stay for two years and hold the Party together while we went about the process of picking a new leader. I sent the piece to the *Globe and Mail* which featured it on their editorial page July 30, two weeks prior to our first post-election caucus.

"If Mr. Stanfield should exit following the August 14 caucus, precipitating an early leadership convention," I wrote, "an emotional maelstrom will engulf the Party, making the 1967 fracas look like a picnic. We are simply not ready, physically, mentally or emotionally, to consider new leadership nationally at this moment. We have everything to lose in long-range planning if R.L.S. says 'to hell with it' and forces us to jump from the frying pan into the fire."

I went on to make the point that the Party ought to concentrate for the next two years on developing new public policies: "All of this will give us a new direction. Then, after we chart a course for ourselves and for Canada, we will be ready to look for a leader who can symbolize our goal and determination in his or her personality." In other words, policy first and then a leader to project it.

Lesson number one. That isn't the way modern politics works, whether we like it or not. The leader is perceived by the media, the party members and the public to be the most important attraction of a party. The party's beliefs come second.

I didn't see that point nearly as clearly in 1974 as I do now. What started the change in my thinking was a letter from Jack Horner a few days after the *Globe and Mail* article appeared. Since I had always regarded our relationship as one of armed neutrality (to be frank about it, I always thought that Horner, a veteran Conservative, resented the fresh image of Alberta that Joe Clark, Harvie Andre and I brought to Parliament in the 1972 election), I was surprised to hear from him. Horner argued that if Stanfield didn't intend to lead us into the next election, he ought to get out now: "You suggest Mr. Stanfield should stay on until the Party can develop a whole new set of policies. A new leader tends to implant his concepts and policies in the Party. During a leadership convention each prospective leader outlines the direction in which he believes his Party and the country should be going. Therefore each prospective leader naturally favours a certain set of policies and, therefore, the establishment of a whole new set of policies before a new leader is chosen would be a complete waste of time."

I guess the chicken does come before the egg. The leader inspires the policy. In any event no policy has much future if the leader doesn't like it.

But who would we like for leader? Since the caucus overwhelmingly felt that no one appealed to us as much as the steady hand of R.L.S., he was given a standing ovation (though there were two or three who remained seated) after telling us that he would continue to serve but no later than the winter of 1976.

Through the winter of 1974-75 the name of Peter Lougheed dominated the mounting speculation. When he called a provincial election for March, five months short of four years in office, many people (myself included) thought that one of the reasons was to set up his own timing for the leadership convention. He would, after all, have nearly a year to set his priorities for Alberta in place before going to Ottawa.

Lougheed's electoral victory (sixty-nine of seventy-five seats) was an overwhelming vote of confidence not only in the man personally but in his ability to deal with Ottawa. I took the view that since the national policies on energy and transportation—the two critical issues in Alberta—were set in Ottawa, not Edmonton, Albertans would be better served by Lougheed as Prime Minister. Not that Lougheed would slant national policies for the direct benefit of Alberta; rather, because he believed in building Confederation out of the regional strengths of Canada, that he would launch energy and transportation policies to build up the regions—and that would also be good for Alberta.

I presented this argument to the annual meeting of my constituency association in Edmonton-Strathcona. Lougheed's proven ability as a manager of government, vote-getter, and communicator made him a natural selection for national leader, I said: "He knows instinctively that the unity of Canada comes out of the harmonizing of diversified regional interests—and is not something forced from the top of a centralized government. Not only Alberta, not only the federal Progressive Conservatives need him, all Canada needs Lougheed."

I could feel the resistance among my own supporters to this argument. Some felt that the Premier should stay in Alberta where he could work more directly for the development of the province, which would mean shifting the economy from dependence on exhaustible oil resources to secondary industry. Besides, why trade his regional power base for an uncertain future as Opposition leader? As usual I was surprised when people didn't agree with my analysis. But I felt public pressure would gradually mount to the point where Lougheed would find the call irresistible.

When the Premier turned up in Halifax where the Conservatives were holding a national caucus and made a speech crammed with Canadianism at a fund-raising dinner, I concluded that he was indicating his availability. Politicians can usually tell—or we think we can—what the real purpose of a speech is. When Lougheed talked about his ancestral roots being in the Maritimes, family values, national goals, national problems and national opportunities, the overall impression was that here was a man of great strength, energy and commitment who already was a national leader.

As I talked to my colleagues in the caucus from Ontario—it is impossible to dispute the fact that Ontario is the key to electoral victory—I became convinced that Lougheed would do well there. The image of "the blue-eyed Arab" from the West would be superseded by a saleable argument that "he fought for Alberta and he'll fight for all Canada."

Of course the Premier kept insisting publicly that he was not interested in the Conservative leadership. But what else could he say, I thought. The moment he indicates interest the convention will be over and whatever he does in Alberta in the interval might be questioned as self-serving. Time, more time was needed.

Just as the summer was getting under way Joe Clark phoned to invite me to a small meeting he was holding in Toronto to examine the viability of his candidacy. I was already out west and told him I couldn't go. Clark said he and his wife Maureen would be going to France for a month where he would immerse himself in the French language.

Lougheed was increasingly on my mind as the summer wore on. One day in August, while I was attending the annual Couchiching

Conference of the Canadian Institute on Public Affairs where I was giving a paper on Canada and the Third World, I received a message that the Premier wanted to see me. A week later I was sitting down to breakfast with him in his office in the Legislature. Confident and relaxed, he seemed in complete control of everything around him. Beside his chair in the study just off his office was a phone panel with a dozen buttons. It seemed to me that we talked of everything under the sun. I was determined not to talk about the leadership until he brought it up so that it would not seem that I was there to pressure him.

Finally he asked me what I thought about the leadership question. I put the argument to him plainly and simply: Canada needed him more than Alberta did—and Albertans would release him from the commitment he had made to Alberta in the March election. I told him I would never accept the argument that he could do more for Alberta in Edmonton than in Ottawa.

Well, he said, he had naturally thought about the matter a great deal and had come to the firm conclusion that he would not run. His commitment to Alberta was too strong. And he wanted me to know his decision.

"What about a draft?" I asked.

A very unlikely possibility, he responded.

Was he thinking of the kind of draft in which every candidate would step aside for him? I thought it was clear that the draft I had in mind was one in which his supporters would lock up a first-ballot victory without his having to campaign for it. I chose not to push him because I did not want to force him into an unequivocal *no* at this point. I left in an ambivalent state of mind. He seemed serious in saying he would not run. He had not said that he would not accept a draft.

When Parliament resumed just after Thanksgiving national attention was focused on the wage-and-price control program that Prime Minister Trudeau had suddenly implemented. But for Tory M.P.s the leadership question had moved into first place on our priority list. It was never discussed in caucus, at least in any substantive way, but it dominated our private conversations.

"Let's have a coffee," I said to Harvie Andre after Question Period on our first day back. We went up to the fifth floor cafeteria in the Centre Block.

"What are we going to do about Lougheed?" I asked.

"We've got to get him," Andre replied.

Lougheed had just completed a heavily publicized business and trade mission through England, Scotland, Belgium, France, Germany and Austria. Had it been a Broadway production it would have been billed a "smash hit." With an entourage of eighty people around him, he charmed everyone he met, projecting a firm image of business decisiveness (as befits a Harvard M.B.A.) mixed with a deepening social concern. The Canadian journalist Christina Newman revealed in her dispatches that she too had been magnetized by the Lougheed "cult."

Andre and I agreed to take two days for a very informal assessment of caucus feelings. No meetings, no pressure, just conversations. When we met again two days later in my office, the message was clear to both of us. The caucus, as a whole, wanted Lougheed. Many were ready to sign a petition to be sent to him; others said they would sign once they were assured of his availability since they did not want to injure relations with declared candidates.

Over the weekend Andre and I put together a Committee of Ten (meant to convey the idea that Lougheed had support in ten provinces, although we had no one from Quebec, a deficiency later remedied by the inclusion of Senator Louis-Phillipe Beaubien). The group* met Monday night in Andre's office and, after thrashing the matter over for two hours, authorized Andre and me to write to the Premier advising him that we intended to launch a national "Draft Lougheed" movement.

The three-page letter, asking for a meeting of the Committee of Ten with Lougheed, centred around this paragraph: "History shows that occasions are few when there is a genuine convergence of the

*Besides Andre and myself there were Ron Huntington, British Columbia, Jim Balfour, Saskatchewan, Jake Epp, Manitoba, Bob Holmes, Ontario, Bob Howie, New Brunswick, Bob Coates, Nova Scotia, Heath Macquarrie, Prince Edward Island, James McGrath, Newfoundland.

need for an individual with the availability of that individual. Such a time is now. Canada needs you at this moment because of your unique ability to produce progressive and unifying policies and build a consensus around them, manage a government apparatus, communicate with the public, both personally and electronically. With the greatest respect we say to you: it is your duty to run for the office of Prime Minister."

Andre and I well recognized that Lougheed didn't need any rhetoric from us. As a very practical politician, he would make up his own mind on an assessment of public and personal facts known to him. But if he were available, then our movement—along with a citizens' draft starting in Toronto—would make it easier for him to declare.

Not the least purpose of the letter was to smoke him out. We told him precisely what we wanted to do—fan out through the provinces, enlisting enough support to ensure a first-ballot victory—so that he could tell us to stop. As long as he knew what we were doing and didn't repudiate our effort, the draft would continue. I went to New York to spend a week at the United Nations as a parliamentary observer. Toward the end of the week Andre phoned to say that Lougheed would see the Group of Ten. The Members were scrambling to adjust their schedules to go to Alberta. It seemed too easy. Surely Lougheed realized that if ten M.P.s turned up in Alberta the national press would be right on to the story. After a few more phone calls the correct message came through: the Premier had meant that he would see Andre and me. I felt it would be better strategy if I held back. On November 7 Andre went alone, was served breakfast, and came away with the impression that the door had not been shut.

Some of the prospective candidates were becoming nervous at this point. They were about to commit large sums of money to their candidacies in the expectation that they had a chance—with Lougheed not running. If Lougheed were running, they would not enter the race. One candidate who did not recognize the Lougheed question mark was Joe Clark. He and Andre and I met the following Saturday in my office and he told us that he would be announcing his candidacy in a few days. Clark was moving ahead because he was convinced that Lougheed would not enter the race in any circumstances.

I could see that Clark wanted our support. But I still thought Lougheed would eventually be available. As for Clark himself, I told him I admired him for running, that he had the qualities of intelligence, drive, and great political ability and that his campaign would set him up beautifully for the next time around. He would come out as an established national figure.

Clark spoke quite clearly. He was not running for the next time. He was running for this time. I didn't want to dispute that point with him because any political campaign is so demanding that the candidate has to have within him a conviction that he is needed and can win. This interior momentum would be needed even more in the warfare of a leadership campaign.

I was in a difficult position. I liked Joe Clark, believed in him and yet felt he didn't have the experience to be leader. I suggested a first-ballot vote without any commitment but then thought he deserved more than such a perfunctory nod. It should be an unequivocal commitment or none at all.

The seriousness of his campaign was evident from his opening announcement in which he called for a turning away from "inappropriate centralization": "We must vest the provinces with the fiscal and political power to nurture vital regional and provincial and local interests, thus encouraging a regionalism that is cheerfully committed to one nation." Clark's emphasis on organization was clear-cut: "Discussion of philosophy is important and so is our performance as an opposition in Parliament. But our essential task is to build a party which can form a national majority government. That requires active organization and a disciplined and united approach."

Clark was a fighter; he would build a solid campaign. I was in a quandary and the Lougheed confusion wasn't helping my thinking. I began to realize that Lougheed, in addition to being good for the country, would ease my personal relations with Clark (as well as other candidates who wanted my support).

My friendship with Clark was not of the same degree as Harvie Andre's (he and Clark had gone to school together and roomed together in Ottawa following the 1972 election). Yet Clark and I got along well, he had visited my home in Edmonton several times and I knew him as well as any M.P. All this was going through my mind when he stopped into my Edmonton office a couple of weeks later. I was uncomfortable and wanted to talk but Joe was in a hurry to catch a plane. We agreed to try to get together soon—but it was the last conversation I had with him until we met briefly the night the convention opened.

Following Andre's breakfast meeting with Premier Lougheed, the Committee of Ten met again, agreed to escalate the pressure, and named the veteran Prince Edward Island M.P. Heath Macquarrie, as our spokesman. In a felicitously phrased news release announcing the Draft Lougheed movement, Macquarrie declared, "Not for a moment would I disparage or express disfavour for those who have so far displayed their high sense of duty in seeking the leadership of the Party." Translated, this meant we were worried that a failed Lougheed draft would tarnish whoever did win as a second-best choice. A feeling was spreading and was openly expressed at a cocktail party we had for the caucus: get Lougheed committed soon or cut loose before we hurt the Party.

The draft was now on the front pages across Canada and Paul Jackson, the parliamentary correspondent for the Edmonton *Journal*, came to see me to get the background story. Then followed one of those politician-newspaperman confrontations about who-said-what. The interview was on the record and I tried to indicate to Jackson the Committee of Ten's basic approach to Lougheed: he had a duty to Canada to run for the office of Prime Minister. The way it came out on the front page of the *Journal* the next day, I was in substance telling Lougheed that he was failing his country by not running. I'm not quarrelling here with Jackson, who is a conscientious newsman. I was probably not careful enough in my language. The point is, I didn't intend to impugn Lougheed's patriotism (hardly a productive approach in persuading him to run).

I couldn't understand a note my secretary gave me during a meeting I was holding with Andre and Macquarrie the next afternoon: "Frank McMillan says to tell you that you are a damn fool for what you said to Paul Jackson about Premier Lougheed." I was puzzling over this when Ian Seph, Lougheed's executive assistant, called to say the Premier was "disturbed" about my comments. When the comments were read to me I was disturbed too. I disclaimed any impugnment of Lougheed's patriotism and sent him my apologies for this embarrassment.

All this, of course, was a side issue. But it revealed the growing tension. The air had to be cleared. The *Journal* accused the Draft Lougheed movement of "a completely unjustifiable sense of desperation" and singled me out as guilty of "extraordinary presumption." Seven weeks later, on January 14, the *Journal* decided there would have to be a Lougheed draft after all and published a rare front-page editorial promoting one. (On the same day the *Globe and Mail* had a lead editorial urging Lougheed to run.) I was glad to see that newspapers, as well as politicians, can change their minds. But by that time most politicians had lost interest; moreover, the declared candidates were forging strong identities in the delegates' minds.

The Draft Lougheed movement ended a few days after the barrage of publicity in mid-November. Macquarrie had been ambivalent about going to Calgary to see the Premier (who had offered a Saturday afternoon appointment on Grey Cup weekend). "I love the West, the man and all sorts of things, but I don't want to fly a few thousand miles for a mere courteous reception, no matter how charming," he told me. It was left that I would attempt to get the definitive answer. Seph arranged for me to see the Premier at 8:15 a.m. Monday in Edmonton so that I could still catch the morning plane to Ottawa.

Lougheed was in a chipper mood, the Eskimos having won the Grey Cup the day before (in a 9-8 squeaker over Montreal). He was sporting an Eskimo victory button on his jacket. I told him I didn't want our personal relations ruined over a quote I had not intended. He said not to worry about it and we settled down into a discussion of the leadership. His feelings had not changed; he was committed to staying in Alberta. He conceded that his advisers were right in telling him he would have to issue an irrevocable statement. It would be out in seventy-two hours, he said. I didn't think there was much more to say; you can only harangue a man so long. We shook hands and I walked out to my car where my son Doug was waiting to drive me to the airport.

"I'm going to tell you something," I said. "Always do what you think is right. That way you can live with yourself longer. It was better to try to get Premier Lougheed and fail than not to have tried." We drove the rest of the way in silence.

Two days later Lougheed issued his statement: "In order to discourage any further efforts to attempt to convince me to alter my position I should . . . state that in the very unlikely event of a so-called 'draft' that I would not accept such an approach."

He followed this up with a letter to Macquarrie who released it to the Group of Ten: "As you are well aware, it was a very difficult decision for me to make. Among other factors, I felt I had to bear in mind the post-Watergate attitude towards political leaders and the cynicism that would have developed—particularly by young Albertans—if I had changed my position."

"Well," I said to Macquarrie, "look at it this way. We did the Party a big favour by settling the Lougheed question early. Now all the candidates know where they stand."

The question, as far as I was concerned, was where did I stand? I didn't want to think about it for awhile and was glad an invitation had come along to go to Ste. Marguerite, Quebec for a four-day conference of development experts from around the world, sponsored by the Canadian International Development Agency.

But the question kept nagging me. When the conference broke into workshops on the third afternoon I went for a long walk through the Laurentian Hills. It was a superb early winter day and the scenery, flecked with a light snowfall, had a calming effect on me. When I returned to my room I got out my leadership file and read all the candidates' statements. As I read Claude Wagner's I thought back to some of my first contacts with him after we had both entered the Commons in 1972.

I had heard of him as a crime-busting crown attorney appointed a judge in the early 1960s, who entered Quebec politics and was soon Minister of Justice. Robert Bourassa had defeated him for leader in 1970 when the delegates-at-large, the appointees of the Quebec Liberal establishment, swung behind Bourassa. Dejected, Wagner had returned to the bench as a sessions court judge only to find himself sought by the federal Tories as a much-needed star Quebec candidate to run in the 1972 election. The Conservatives did poorly in that election, winning only three of the seventy-four seats in Quebec and Wagner came to Ottawa realizing that his political coat-tails were non-existent (although the popular vote did improve for the Conservatives).

His first major speech on Canada's peace-keeping role in Vietnam had been a commanding performance and revealed a sensitivity obscured by his hard-line image dating back to his days as a judge. His colleagues looked on him as a leader.

When I made my "New West" speech in 1973, declaring that the New West supports the principle of one Canada requiring the maintenance of a partnership of equality between English and French, Wagner congratulated me warmly. (The speech upset some of my western colleagues who didn't like my implication that all modern westerners support bilingualism.) Wagner began to tease me about the New West and we developed an easy relationship that was intensified as I gradually shifted my attention to external affairs, of which he was caucus chairman.

When the External Affairs Subcommittee on International Development was set up, Wagner asked me to take charge of it for our party and said he would stand behind whatever I recommended. I'm human enough, I think, to appreciate a vote of confidence in my judgment and ability. When Wagner came West in the fall of 1973 on a speaking tour I had a reception for him in my home and was glad to see the warm feelings he generated among my friends.

I often felt that he should exert himself more strongly both in caucus and in the House. On the other hand, whenever he spoke in either place, I noticed how carefully everyone listened. His judgment was always apparent. The most memorable display of this was during the acrimonious days of the bilingualism debate of 1973 when our caucus was divided and Stanfield's efforts to unify us were being thwarted by our more recalcitrant colleagues. Wagner, in complete control of himself, displayed patience and moderation and when he spoke he said he would go on respecting all his colleagues just as he hoped they would respect him. He could easily have fractured an already polarized caucus but he chose to be himself an instrument of unity. I liked that.

What I didn't like was the handling of a $300,000 trust fund set up for Wagner. The origins of this fund are in the files and memories of a handful of key individuals: Robert Stanfield, Finlay MacDonald, Stanfield's chief-of-staff at the time of Wagner's entry into the Party, Brian Mulroney, the Montreal lawyer who first brought Stanfield and Wagner together and who later was to become Wagner's nemesis, and Eddie Goodman, the Toronto lawyer and fund-raiser for the Party.

The tales of meetings, discussions and arrangements have taken on the air of intrigue for what should have been a straightforward business deal. In 1972 Wagner was being asked to shoulder extra responsibilities for the development of the Party in Quebec; he would be leaving a job with security (he has a wife and three teen- and college-aged children) for the hazards of being a Tory politician in Quebec. Why should there not be a fund to help him? King, St. Laurent and Pearson had all had funds to supplement their income as politicians. The funds made it possible for all three to stay in politics and no one has ever suggested that they acted improperly or gave special treatment to their benefactors. Stanfield himself has said, "It's not an unusual thing for men entering public life, or for people wanting to stay in public life, to have some financial arrangement."

Stanfield maintained that he did not handle the details of the Wagner fund but left the impression that Party funds were at least partly used to set up the fund which Wagner says provides an income of $12,000 a year, after taxes. Before compulsory disclosure was instituted by the 1974 federal campaign law, party finances were "a pretty highly confidential matter."

"It wouldn't have surprised me to learn that some kind of fund had been established in connection with Mr. Wagner," Stanfield told a Standard Broadcast News reporter on November 12 before the convention. "I assumed it was quite a move for him to leave a secure position to return to all the vagaries of politics and continue after the election in that kind of a doubtful position."

The reporter, Brian Nelson, then asked him, "What about other M.P.s and defeated candidates who joined the Party in the hopes of winning a seat in the 1972 election and did not receive money?"

Stanfield replied, "Well, you know, all candidates are not in the same position . . . I happen to think that it's been very important for the Party that Claude Wagner remain in our ranks, remain as a prominent Quebecer in our Party. I think it's important that he be able to do that and maintain his family obligations."

The sensitivity of the Party officials to possible criticism from within the Party doubtless led to the decision to keep the fund secret. Moreover, the existence of the fund would have become an issue in the 1972 election because our opponents would have charged us with "buying" Quebec support. Trying to put out the rumours, Wagner, on September 5, 1972 just as the campaign was starting, denied that there was a fund. Although he did not begin to receive income from the fund until after the election, the denial returned later to haunt Wagner. The publicity led Paul Hellyer to question "the reasons why newspapers, that have been aware of the fund for months or years, waited until this particular moment when the February leadership convention approached to publish the facts. And why are some of the same people who were so anxious to recruit Wagner in 1972 allegedly so anxious to cooperate with the press now in creating a storm?" Hellyer added, in one of his last columns before plunging into the leadership race himself, "Wagner deserves better treatment. Whenever I am asked why there are not really more outstanding men in politics, I cite this kind of machination as one of the most important reasons."

So the Wagner fund, I concluded that afternoon in Ste. Marguerite, should not be a factor in my decision. I myself had received $10,000 in cash from Party funds in each of my two elections as campaign contributions and a subsidy for my constituency office.

There was nothing unethical about this. Nobody was questioning my honesty. Why should Wagner's be questioned?

I turned back to the speech he had made in announcing his candidacy and found it surprisingly populist. He had committed himself to relying on the democratic structures of the Party as a primary step in bringing about true national unity based on linguistic equality and partnership: "I abhor the concept of leadership which, unconcerned with the majority's wishes, would be undermined by behind-the-scenes brokers, puppeteers, back-room schemers, more preoccupied with perpetuating past quarrels than in working for the common good, and selfishly profiting by their secret influence. The era for vendettas is over. Personally I have worked, am working and will continue to work to rid our Party of all trace and memory of such battles. I want to unify the Party, not divide it. I am a member of no clan and no camp!" (The allusion in the last word of that sentence was fairly clear; hence it was no surprise that Dalton Camp later excoriated Wagner, claiming he was going hard-line on —of all subjects—bilingualism.)

Without the support of Quebec, Wagner warned, Progressive Conservatives might just as well accept that they will remain the ongoing Opposition at the national level. The profile of the whole Party must be raised within Quebec: "I am a candidate set at winning, to enable the Conservative Party to carry out the dreams of so many generations of Quebecers to have the Progressive Conservative Party choose a Francophone leader, not merely because he is from Quebec, not for the mere sake of sordid electoral calculations, but because I feel more than anybody else, I am best able to help Canada survive in the unity and diversity our founders dreamed to be hers."

When I read this I remembered a comment Stanfield had made at a press conference following the 1974 election. After making clear that he wasn't endorsing anyone, he said, "I think it would be a good idea for the Progressive Conservative Party to have a French-Canadian leader, a leader from the province of Quebec, but it'll be for the Party to make that decision."

The mood of the Party in 1976 is slightly to the right of the political centre. ("I am in the extreme centre," I always tell friends.) But, in fact, I felt that Wagner's economic and social views did reflect the moderation necessary to relate to a conservative political climate. That, plus his ability to serve as a mediating factor between Quebec and the rest of Canada. I thought he needed westerners like myself to exert an influence on him, and who might, in turn, be able to help him in western Canada.

I was worried about the capital punishment issue, since Wagner, unlike myself, was committed to the principle of retention, but I had immediately to weigh it against the abortion issue. Both in public and private Wagner had made clear his opposition to abortion and I was very impressed by the depth of his anti-abortion feeling.

The afternoon was wearing on and the Laurentian Hills were already lost in the early darkness of December as I looked out the hotel window. I poured a drink and paced my room.

Wagner or Clark? Quebec or Alberta? Experience or freshness? Which one?

They both wanted me. Not that I'm invaluable. But candidates need Members backing them.

Sit on the fence. Wait to see what happens. Don't jump too soon. Smart politicians wait. Not many M.P.s in the caucus are committed. Why should you be?

Because I hate fence-sitters and opportunists waiting to move to the sure winner. I've always stuck my neck out in politics. Bilingualism, abortion, foreign aid, immigration. Why not leadership?

Because it's dangerous. Whole careers are involved in this one. You guess wrong and—zap.

But that's what's wrong with politics. You calculate all the odds before you move in order to get on the winning track. What kind of leadership is that?

Quebec doesn't trust the Conservative Party. That's not my fault but maybe I can do something about it.

Can Wagner win the West? Certainly. The West is so Conservative that the political momentum will overpower anti-French feelings.

What about Alberta? Can I bring my own delegates with me?

Why worry? Albertans will divide between Horner and Clark on the first ballot. When Horner and Clark are eliminated they'll go to Wagner—if we prepare the way and open the doors. Why fight the delegates at this stage?

Will Clark move to Wagner in the later stages? I think he will.

Wait. No. Clark wants an answer from me. If I keep him waiting I'm fence-sitting.

Clark or Wagner?

God, why did I get into politics? How to lose friends. Why didn't I get a job as a convention official so I would have to remain neutral? Stall. No.

Clark's young. He's got time.

Wagner gets it now or he's out.

What's best for the country? How do I know?

Wagner this time.

Clark next time.

Wagner.

In Ottawa a few days later I went to see Wagner. He guaranteed me a free vote on capital punishment. I didn't raise the abortion issue. We talked about unifying the caucus and the Party. He seemed really pleased when I told him I would support him and asked me to announce my decision.

I called Clark's office so that I could see him before the announcement came out but he was out west and wouldn't be back until after I had gone to Edmonton for the Christmas recess. I wrote a lengthy letter to him: "I have told you before that I have strong feelings favourable to yourself. It goes without saying that I value your friendship. That has made this problem all the more difficult. But having sent all the relevant material through my mental process I have come down on the side of Claude Wagner."

How would Edmonton-Strathcona delegates take my decision, I wondered. Perhaps I should have consulted them? Oh hell, this decision was so tough, I don't want to argue with anyone. Anyway, I rationalized, they knew I was thinking about Wagner. I prepared a news release for the Edmonton media and timed it for January 2.

I supported Wagner, the release said, because of his judgment and moderation as well as his commitment to true national unity in Canada, "a unity that comes through economic and social policies as well as linguistic and cultural." As the weeks passed I realized that this endorsement inadequately represented my true feelings on the Quebec factor in Wagner's candidacy. Of course, it would hardly do to declare support on racial grounds. Yet something more needed to be said. I was glad therefore when the Toronto *Globe and Mail* political columnist Geoffrey Stevens came to see me about why I was supporting Wagner. In a relaxed conversation with him I found the right words which he accurately conveyed to his readers.

Intelligence, strength and moderation. These were the qualities I sought, along with the ability to unify the Conservative caucus and the Quebec factor, Stevens reported: "When such a person comes on the national scene with a broad background of political, judicial and ministerial experience, then I think to reject him would be to tell the people of Quebec: 'Look, no matter what your attributes are, you can't make it all the way in the Tory Party and the very best you can do is the Quebec lieutenancy'—which by its very nature implies a second-class citizenry."

In short, the Wagner candidacy offered us a chance to repudiate forever the idea that the Conservative Party is the preserve of English-speaking commercial interests. Obviously it would be going too far to state that a Wagner victory was essential to this process. There were many Conservatives within Quebec—including some very important ones—who opposed Wagner because they didn't think he was the man for the job.

The candidacy of Brian Mulroney, the Montreal lawyer and long-time Conservative back-room worker, mystified me. He had brought Wagner into the Party and now was locked in warfare with him over Quebec delegates. The internecine battle was too much to figure out and I put Mulroney's entry down to a strong ego that might in the long run totally damage Wagner's aspirations as a French Canadian. Of all the serious candidates running, the only one I was opposed to—and strongly—was Brian Mulroney, because he had never been elected to anything. I figured that I had more right to the leadership than he did; at least I had been elected twice.

When I arrived home Christmas was in full swing and I didn't want to talk politics. The family had a five-day vacation planned for Jasper and we went off on the train in a happy mood, looking forward to being together, skiing, skating and playing bridge. When we met friends I tried to avoid politics but it was difficult. Interest in the Conservative convention was picking up. When we arrived home Eva read about my Wagner decision in the paper and was hurt that I hadn't discussed it with her. She favoured Clark and though would have respected (if not agreed with) my reasoning, felt left out. I realized I had handled this the wrong way.

Again I put the matter out of my mind because I had to get ready for a national speaking tour. With Andrew Brewin of the N.D.P. and Irénée Pelletier of the Liberals, I had agreed to go across Canada for ten days speaking about Canada's role in international development. I was in the middle of writing a speech when Rich Willis, a campaign organizer for Wagner, phoned from Toronto to ask if I would set up a program for Wagner's visit to Edmonton the following week during a western swing. Although I would be away on tour, I agreed to help. Ross Rigney, one of my political supporters, had told me after the Wagner announcement that he was enthusiastic about my decision. I called Ross and he agreed to handle arrangements. Darryl Smith would set up a press conference. My secretary Betty Mitchell, also a delegate to the convention who was meeting all the candidates, sent out invitations to a reception.

From the reports I received, Wagner was well received both by the media and the delegates at the Edmonton reception on January 13.

On January 10, flying from Edmonton to Halifax, I picked up the *Globe and Mail*. There on the front page was a major story by Jonathan Manthorpe on "the wooing of Wagner," giving all the details of how Wagner was brought into the Conservative Party—and the outline of how the fund was set up. The conflict between the precise date of the fund's beginning and Wagner's denial of it on September 5, 1972 was still unresolved. The principals in the arrangement weren't talking, leaving the impression that they were protecting themselves. The setting up of the fund had been handled badly and Wagner was the one now exposed. Obviously the *Globe and Mail* piece would spread a cloud of uncertainty about Wagner's integrity. But I felt he was being victimized, unable to speak in his own defence without damaging others who were not properly authorized by the party executive to set up the fund in the first place.

The net effect of all this was to build the fund as an issue of increasing interest to the media, thus diverting Wagner at press conferences from projecting his message on the campaign issues. A defensive candidate is not a good candidate. As I moved west myself, reading the press reports in the wake of Wagner's tour, I realized he was in trouble. Back in Ottawa a reception for Ottawa-area delegates was held in the Railway Committee room of the Parliament Buildings on January 29. Wagner's speech was strong, the crowd responsive and the M.P.s appeared impressed. The question period opened and a journalist immediately tossed a hostile question to him on the fund. In an emotional moment Wagner pointed to his wife and children near him and denied that there was anything improper in the fund. As the family pictures were being shot afterwards, the candidate smiled, but he was not happy.

Nonetheless his campaign was building. The Montreal *Star* reported that Wagner emerged as the headliner in an all-candidates' meeting in Halifax. Bill Johnson of the *Globe and Mail* wrote that "a great number of delegates could live with Mr. Wagner." But on the whole the press coverage tended to diminish the stature of Wagner. Compared with the effusive and adulatory profile of Mulroney, a candidate whose well-financed style obscured any substance, it was a sad reflection of the irresponsible bandwagon style of much of the media. What counted, of course, was what the delegates, not the media, thought of Wagner. But at a meeting of M.P.s supporting Wagner the negative influence of the media was recognized. Wagner would certainly start the balloting well but victory was far from sure. Speculation arose that he might not be able to grow sufficiently during the balloting.

The next week Wagner called me from Toronto to ask if I would accompany him on a four-day campaign tour in the West to reach areas he had not previously visited. I realized he needed moral support and agreed. We would meet in Toronto the following Wednesday morning. On Saturday evening I made a quick trip back to Edmonton because my daughter Mary Anne was having her sixteenth birthday; I spent all day Saturday writing and once aboard the plane settled down with the newspapers.

Two weeks before balloting, and there was the fund back on the front page of the Toronto *Star*, this time in a story by Robert McKenzie quoting Peter White, a former Wagner aide, who claimed that a large sum of cash had been delivered to Wagner's home before the 1972 election. One had to read to the sixteenth paragraph to get a vehement denial of this by Eddie Goodman, one of the key figures in organizing the fund. "No money from the fund was ever given to anybody during the year 1972," Goodman told the *Star* reporter. "That is the largest lie. The last time he [White] said that, he said that the money from the fund was delivered and that is an outright prevarication."

Le Devoir that day was also pressing the fund story and a long front-page article centred on the question of whether Wagner had told the truth. And why would he not tell everything about the fund?

I spent the weekend brooding about this instead of enjoying my daughter's birthday. On Monday morning, before flying back to Ottawa, I went into the health club at the Y.M.C.A. for a workout— and there it was again. The Calgary *Albertan* had a front page headline: "Mysterious Wagner income raises suspicions." The issue was now clearly the integrity of Wagner. It would kill his candidacy unless this cloud could be lifted. Although he ought never to have allowed himself to be trapped, it was now too late for Wagner to defend himself. (Some M.P.s were saying they wouldn't support him solely on the grounds of his mishandling of the fund information, which indicated to them that if Wagner couldn't handle this crisis, he couldn't cope with the constant pressure and demands of the leadership.)

Sitting in the steam bath, I determined that Stanfield would have to help—not help Wagner's campaign but help to remove the suspicions which were developing into such an unfair disadvantage. I wrapped a towel around myself and phoned Paul Weed, Wagner's campaign manager, Elmer MacKay, Jack Ellis and Paul Dick, three of Wagner's M.P. supporters. There was a general agreement that we would have to see Stanfield. An appointment was made for the following morning.

There were eight in the small delegation* that walked into the leader's fourth-floor office in the Centre Block the next day. Several of us spoke, emphasizing that the name of Wagner had to be cleared. Stanfield expressed concern but advised caution, lest any statement by himself at this stage cause the whole situation to blow up and create the impression that he was siding with Wagner's political candidacy. I argued that a way could be found to clear Wagner's integrity without backing his campaign. Stanfield wanted to keep thinking about the situation.

The next morning I met Wagner in a hangar at Toronto airport where an executive jet, loaned to him by Steven Roman, chairman of the board of Denison Mines and unsuccessful Conservative candidate in the 1974 election, was waiting. The plane had been used by Sinclair Stevens in his leadership campaign travels and I didn't see anything wrong with a campaign donation by Roman in the form of four days' free travel. Wagner, in a great coonskin coat, was reasonably relaxed. He had been so upset at the previous Saturday's bad publicity that he had scrapped a weekend trip to the Maritimes. Campaigning was no longer fun, his wife and family were upset at the constant innuendoes, and the strain was clearly showing on his face.

I was glad that Jack Ellis and Bob Geddes were coming with us. Former mayor of Belleville and Member for Hastings, Ellis always seems to maintain a contagious air of exuberance. Geddes, a worker in the Weed campaign organization, is calm and efficient.

A couple of hours later we were in the Mystery Lake Motor Inn in Thompson, Manitoba, 500 miles north of Winnipeg. The delegates of the riding of Churchill had gathered over sandwiches and coffee. Wagner chatted easily with them and they warmed to him.

*Bob McCleave and Elmer MacKay, Nova Scotia; Jack Ellis and Paul Dick, Ontario; John Reynolds, British Columbia; Senator Jacques Flynn and Jacques Lavoie, Quebec; and myself.

Their questions focused on strikes in the public service, bilingualism and how the Conservatives could build strength in Quebec. The sun was shining brilliantly as we swept over the lakes and trees into a faultless blue sky. Wagner's confidence was coming back.

In Winnipeg the CTV, CBC, Toronto *Star* and Montreal *Star* were waiting along with the local press. Ordinarily this kind of attention is what candidates crave. But the national reporters were not interested in covering Wagner's campaign as such. They wanted to see how much the fund was hurting him; their attitude was conditioned by the speculation that Wagner's campaign was falling apart.

A coffee party was set up in the International Inn to give delegates a chance to talk to Wagner. In order to show that Wagner was not a remote statesman who only made speeches, the western tour had been designed to provide informal, come-and-go meetings with delegates. Two coffee parties had been organized at the homes of Annas Shaddy and Elizabeth Wilcox for the evening. The afternoon session was at an awkward hour, unfortunately. Only five delegates came and the low number was emphasized in the news reports. The cameras and microphones bore in on Wagner talking to this small group and what was to be intimate conversation became contrived and artificial.

The four of us ate a glum dinner in Wagner's room, listening to the *World at Six* boost Mulroney. When I returned to my room I discovered that a water main had broken, shutting off water in the hotel. This didn't help my mood but I used the water in the toilet box for shaving, and told my unshaven colleagues when we met downstairs that this campaign required a great deal of adaptability.

The object of the tour, Ellis and I agreed, was to provide the opportunity of forging a bond between candidate and delegates and this couldn't be done with hostile media intruders making everyone nervous. Whether the managers back at headquarters agreed or not, we recognized that Wagner would not be able to function while he was being harassed. So we cut out the media and held closed sessions. The two evening coffee parties provided crowded living rooms and Wagner performed well. When the fund question came up, he handled it easily, making two essential points: Stanfield and Mulroney were the ones who had all the answers and he, Wagner, was proud to receive financial support in order for the public to know that one does not have to be independently wealthy to progress in politics. I sat in a corner taking all this in, wishing the press were there to convey the spirit of both meetings. Meanwhile Ellis was upstairs on the phone to Paul Weed who said that his poll showed Wagner winning on the third ballot; however, there were definite signs of slippage in Ontario because of the fund. Could we keep the pressure on Stanfield to make a statement?

The runway at Yorkton, Saskatchewan, was covered with drifting snow the next morning so we immediately diverted to Prince Albert. With the extra time Geddes informed the Chamber of Commerce president that Wagner would be available if they wanted him to express a greeting at their luncheon. An invitation was extended and he spoke a few words, paying tribute to John Diefenbaker who twenty years earlier had set out from Prince Albert to do what Wagner was now doing. The Toronto *Star's* Robert McKenzie, who now was clearly tailing us, reported that Wagner had "crashed" the luncheon, so desperate was he to garner support. There were only two or three delegates on hand to meet Wagner and again the press dwelled on his failure to attract.

Meanwhile I was on the phone to Stanfield, telling him that in our opinion the situation had reached a dangerously high point. Flora MacDonald was now calling for an investigation of the fund. Stanfield advised Claude to stay cool, that the latest round of charges might produce sympathy for him. Still concerned that a statement at this point would escalate the issue even further, Stanfield said he would keep an open mind. I understood the importance to Stanfield of staying above the political battle but I disagreed with his decision to stay above the ethical cloud also. I had long since learned to trust Stanfield's judgment. Was he right this time, too?

There was no time to brood. We moved off to Saskatoon, then Regina for more meetings with delegates. The national reporters kept nagging us. But the meetings were going well and Wagner was making friends. In Regina his confidence came back as he felt the response of the delegates. To try to keep the press happy and because Wagner headquarters was calling for more television exposure,

Ellis and I agreed to an on-the-record interview when the delegates left. The first two questions were: Who does the plane belong to? When did you get cash from the fund? Wagner's irritation showed and the press loved it. Back on the plane Wagner's mood was as black as the sky outside.

The news the next morning in Calgary was that John Turner had resigned his seat in the Commons. Why right before the Conservative leadership campaign? To help Hellyer, who lived in Turner's riding and needed a seat? Eldon Woolliams announced his support of Wagner at a breakfast meeting to which the media had been invited. Wagner, feeling better, made a speech on bilingualism in which he scorned forced bilingualism. "I seek to remove the suspicion and distrust that forced language instruction can create," he said. "I seek to make merit the one criterion for promotion in our public service. I seek to ensure the rights of no group at the expense of any other." The delegates applauded enthusiastically. The T.V. media wanted to do an interview. But it wasn't Wagner's view on bilingualism the reporters wanted but his reaction to Flora MacDonald's statement that the fund should be cleared up. Geddes jumped in and told Claude he had to hurry to his next appointment—which led Claude Arpin of the Montreal *Star* to write that Ellis, Geddes and I were shielding Wagner. This statement led the headline writer to proclaim: "Wagner dances sidestep."

In Edmonton, following a noon-hour session with delegates (many of whom he had not met on his first visit), Wagner heard about the bad press in the East. The good effect he was having on western delegates was clearly being negated by stories that created the impression in eastern minds that he was doing poorly. Again his morale and confidence were in bad shape. I tried to encourage him by telling him that the Clark supporters liked him and would move to him when the time came. Elmer MacKay phoned from Nova Scotia with good reports and that cheered him up.

I went home to spend an hour with my family. We sat in the living room upstairs looking at the sunset across the park. Everything looked better from that perspective. I returned to the hotel in time to catch a local T.V. news report which gave an excellent account of

Wagner's bilingualism speech. Then we were off to Grande Prairie for a wine and cheese party and ended the day in Victoria. The CTV news report on his western tour was positive. And this helped to bolster his morale for a full Saturday of campaigning in Victoria, Campbell River, Kelowna and Prince George. By the time we arrived in Kelowna he was at his peak, charming, satisfying and winning delegates. I saw two women jostle each other to get a seat next to him.

"You're going to win," I said to him in the plane. "Do you think you could give your speech to the convention without notes—just standing there and really communicating with the people the way you do at coffee parties?"

Wagner seemed uncomfortable with the idea. Most of all he was tired. A snowstorm had delayed us in Prince George. It would be 3 a.m. when we landed in Montreal. A final day of campaigning in Quebec lay ahead.

On Sunday at the Wagner campaign headquarters in Ottawa I gave Weed the pluses and minuses on the trip. He was buoyant—but I learned long ago that if campaign managers aren't buoyant they shouldn't be campaign managers. On my way out I stopped to talk to Paul Dick and just then the CBC reporter Mike Duffy called Dick looking for comment on Stanfield's refusal to accede to the M.P.s' request for a statement on Wagner. The visit to Stanfield's office had leaked; the situation would now be worse if the story became Stanfield's refusal to clear Wagner's name. Duffy used the story on the *World at Eight* the next morning. Elmer MacKay and I decided on a final appeal to Stanfield, who agreed to send an emissary to Duffy to tell him that Stanfield had already said several times that there was nothing wrong in having a fund, and that he wasn't going to make any more direct statements.

I missed the *World at Six* because we were voting in the House but caught it at eight o'clock by calling home. Duffy had not used anything more on the story—and the rest of the media hadn't bothered to pursue it. Maybe Stanfield was right. Maybe.

At a Wagner organization meeting on Tuesday, Weed, who had insisted all along that Wagner would have 600 votes on the first ballot, said "the most pessimistic evaluation is 555 votes." Hellyer and Stevens would come to Wagner. And that would do it.

The mail was piled high on my desk and I decided I'd better go through it before the convention started. I had sent out an appeal for funds for the Wagner campaign. "Contrary to media reports," I said in my letter, "Claude Wagner has very limited funds." I wasn't surprised at the light financial response. What did bother me was a number of correspondents opposed to a Quebecer leading the Conservative Party. "Any candidate from Quebec will not draw votes from other parts of Canada," one writer said. "To elect a leader from Quebec is not the answer." Other letters were critical of Wagner over the fund issue. Some of the mail was, of course, complimentary to Wagner. But there were enough negatives on the French Canadian and fund issues to add to my concern.

Stanfield came to his final caucus as leader on Wednesday, talking more about the future than the past. He said he expected us to prove worthy of the heavy responsibility we had as caucus members. There wasn't a leadership candidate in sight. That evening Eva and I had a cocktail party for our Ottawa and Edmonton friends. Mary Dantzer, wife of the former mayor of Edmonton and now a lawyer in Vernon, B.C., was an uncommitted voting delegate. "You're the most important person in town," I told her as I introduced her to the journalists at the party. John Grace, editor of the Ottawa *Journal*, said he couldn't make up his mind about Wagner or Clark and predicted them both on the final ballot. "That's the one scenario that bothers me most about this whole business," I responded. "It's one thing not to support Clark, but I don't want ever to have to vote directly against him."

On Thursday I took the Edmonton-Strathcona delegates to lunch in the parliamentary restaurant, which was so jammed we nearly didn't get in. A foretaste of the crowds pushing and shoving for the next four days, I thought, without the slightest bit of enthusiasm. This was another side of politics, or I should say the tip of the iceberg, the part everyone sees. The banners, the images, the frenzy. Politics as carnival. What a way to choose the leader of the country. And why should people who very often have nothing to do with the regular business and policies of the Party suddenly be given the same vote for leader as one who has himself been elected to caucus and spends every day in the business? Oh, Oh! My elitism is showing again. Too bad, that's the way I feel. Media madness inflates and deflates candidates without any real sense of responsibility and the crowds get swept along. I'm not arguing for a return to the smoke-filled backroom, just for less crowd manipulation by organizers more versed in psychology than philosophy.

Not much of a mood to start the convention in. I held a short meeting with Hugh Segal, a fascinating young assistant to Premier Davis in Toronto who ran unsuccessfully twice for the federal Conservatives in Ottawa Centre. Segal had previously assisted Wagner in his office and was back in Ottawa to help in the campaign. We talked about ways we could help Claude get into final shape for the four policy sessions Friday on external affairs, social order, the economy and political structures. I went to Wagner's office to join the other M.P.s going out to the Civic Centre early. I still wasn't registered and we'd heard about the long lineups.

Elmer MacKay and I took Wagner backstage to wait for the proceedings to begin. He described himself as "serene but fighting." He looked rested and fashionable in a brown checked suit, in contrast to his competitors who all chose dark blue in what appeared to be a sartorial bow to the high moment. When Mulroney came into the room, I noticed Wagner tighten. In other circumstances I would probably have liked this jovial Irishman. But I didn't like him tonight. He belongs with the organizers, not the candidates, I said to myself, shaking hands with him in my best political manner.

I told Clark that he had run a great campaign and Alberta was really proud of him. He was gracious enough—and professional enough—not to remind me that I hadn't been much help to him.

I went out to find Eva and some place to sit. Wandering across the floor I bumped into Finlay MacDonald who began talking about Geoffrey Stevens' *Globe and Mail* column in which I had criticized the organizers of the Wagner fund for not having gone through the Party executive. MacDonald now lives in Florida and this was the first time I had seen him in a couple of years.

"You know," he said, "there were twelve people involved in the fund and it had to be kept private. Some day I'd like to tell you about it."

The crowd was pushing by us and this was hardly the place for an intimate conversation.

"Well, the twelve of you—whoever you are—took one hell of a risk with Wagner's career and maybe the future of the Party in Quebec," I said. "I hope it doesn't boomerang on you on Sunday."

"I think he'll be O.K.," MacDonald said, drifting into the crowd.

The evening belonged to John Diefenbaker. I could hardly believe my ears when he said, "Stanfield was right," referring to the R.L.S. wage-and-price control stand in the 1974 election. More public support earlier in the game might have changed the scoreboard. When Diefenbaker gave a long passage in French, I interpreted this as being helpful to Wagner, even though the Chief would probably support Horner on at least the first ballot.

I was supposed to be on duty at Wagner's hospitality suite at the Skyline. But it, as well as the rest of the hotel, was a flowing mob scene. I left early and down in the lobby stopped for a moment to listen to the Climax Jazz Band blasting away on behalf of Jim Gillies. Jim and his wife Betsy were smiling and tapping away, although I didn't get the feeling he had his heart in it.

Friday morning the M.P.s in chef's attire were serving breakfast to the delegates at the Skyline. I hate wearing funny hats and went up to Wagner's suite to see if he needed help. He asked me to work with Segal in the briefings before each session. The candidates were rotating through the policy sessions and Wagner had the first slot in the external affairs section. He gave a long speech because he wanted to get his ideas out in this area he was most familiar with. He came out for NATO, against a false spirit of *détente* and against the sale of nuclear reactors. Time ran out before questions could start so I suggested that in his next session on social order, he go right into questions, since people generally knew where he stood on law and order. The questions ranged from unemployment insurance to conditions in prisons to violence on television. He was coming through well but earned the most applause at the final session on political structures when he begged delegates not to mistake him for the same kind of French Canadian as Prime Minister Trudeau: "My commitment is to bridge the differences caused by a bilingual program which was enforced without justice, without compassion."

Moving through the hallways I picked up good reports of Flora MacDonald and Joe Clark's performances. "They really know the issues," an Ontario delegate said.

The evening was devoted to the Party's farewell to Stanfield who rose to the occasion with a speech many wished he had made on entering rather than leaving the leadership. Stop the internal fighting or forget about winning elections, he said. And stop the alienation of a quarter of the population of the country: "Let's be frank and honest with ourselves. If Sir John A. is watching us tonight he must be sad indeed to see the small number of Progressive Conservative Francophone Members of Parliament here today."

Stanfield was introduced by Peter Lougheed who spoke graciously but made no attempt to excite the convention that could, a couple of months earlier, have been his. Richard Quittenton, a political unknown who was the twelfth registered candidate, came over to Wagner's box to state that following his speech tomorrow he would drop out of the race and declare for Wagner. The two men shook hands and I looked around in vain for a photographer. "Where are these guys when you want them?" I asked.

I went to the Skyline hospitality suite again and then left to meet Wagner in Segal's room at the Holiday Inn. We had scheduled a run-through of the next day's speech. We timed Wagner at nine minutes and fifty seconds and he decided to put a little more material in it. None of us had had dinner and room service warned of an hour's delay. I got the manager on the phone. "Don't you think Claude Wagner deserves some food after all he's been through today?" I pleaded. Club sandwiches appeared in ten minutes. It was 1 a.m. when we broke up.

"And above all, don't listen to rumours—unless they're ours." The crowd in Wagner's campaign headquarters laughed at Paul Weed's instructions at the Saturday morning meeting. He had the workers in a good mood. Darryl Smith, my campaign manager in

Edmonton-Strathcona, had signed on as a Wagner floorworker and he agreed that it all looked good. We left to go to the caucus of Alberta's 250 delegates, the third largest contingent.

All the candidates came through, giving short speeches. All were politely received with the most applause going to Clark, Horner and Wagner. Lougheed, of course, was staying non-commital. He was quoted afterwards as saying that not even his wife knew how he voted.

Wagner wanted more run-throughs of his speech so Segal and I met him in his office. I paced the floor as I listened to him, from time to time suggesting a bit more passion, especially when he was to say: "I ask that you give a thought to the unity of this party and of this nation." The theme of the speech was unity and it needed to evoke an emotional response. The timing was now thirteen minutes and forty-five seconds, leaving six minutes for Elmer MacKay's introduction and getting on and off the stage. Weed had decided against a band; the M.P.s flanking him on the walk to the stage would be his only accompaniment.

Wagner went home to change. I went to the Civic Centre. The chanting and banner waving of the supporters of all the candidates was almost hysterical. The entire arena seemed to be swaying. It was a moment of frightening intensity.

Then the crowd settled down and John Fraser of Vancouver led off with a workmanlike speech. Mulroney's speech fell flat. Clark and his wife arrived at the podium in an open Landau carriage as a band played "I'se d'bye." A neat entry, I thought, full of style. But his speech seemed hurried. Wagner had the attention of the entire crowd. He was rising to the occasion. Hellyer made a mysterious reference to Red Tories, which was immediately interpreted as a divisive tactic when the crowd wanted unity. When the speeches were finally finished I felt that Wagner had been the strongest performer. He had touched people. Tomorrow would be his.

At the Skyline the crowd in the hospitality suite now stretched down the corridor. The police had arrived to direct traffic. The columnists were on hand for the background story. There was a general assumption, almost something tangible in the warmth of the handshakes, that Wagner was the winner. When he arrived, moving slowly (even regally, some said), he looked the winner.

After he left I went down to the Chateau Laurier where an even bigger Wagner rally was in full swing. The Quebec supporters had joy on their faces. I met some of the reporters who had been hostile to us on the western trip; now they seemed anxious to get the best facts and quotes. I spotted one of the women who had been at one of the Winnipeg coffee parties. "Listen," she said, "I'm going Wagner, but do you know how tough it is for me to vote for a French Canadian to head my Conservative Party?" I figured, when you've made the sale, don't argue, and decided to go home. One of Ottawa's famous February snow storms was raging and taxis were almost as valuable as votes.

At Wagner headquarters the Sunday morning meeting was restrained but confident. One of my M.P. colleagues came over to me. "Do you think," he asked, "that Claude should meet his caucus Monday or wait for the regular Wednesday meeting?" Willis was bellowing out instructions to line captains, the right and wrong way to solicit votes. Hellyer's strange overnight letter to delegates, stating his anti-Red Tory remarks "were not a slip of the tongue nor an ill-considered accident," puzzled everyone. I was glad Darryl and his friend Don Clarke from Edmonton were with me. My back was starting to pain me and I knew I wouldn't be able to stand in the voting lines all day; they agreed to help.

The arena was quiet when I arrived. But as the gladiators took their places the shouts erupted again. The floor was a mass of mouth-to-ear consultations. Somebody told me that Harvie Andre was looking for me. I had not seen Harvie very much since the Lougheed draft fizzled out. He had chosen Clark and was managing the Clark team at the convention. I went to the Clark section at the other end of the arena, dominated by the Clark yellow and black colours that stood out so effectively against the red, white and blue in the rest of the arena. Andre and I went behind the stands to talk. He was confident, he said, showing me the yellow Clark scarves that would be passed around. If Wagner should falter, he wanted me to know I'd be welcome. I decided not to press him. It just seemed obvious to me that if Joe should fade, Harvie would support the leading candidate on the right. That would be Wagner. As for Joe himself, I was positive he would move to Wagner if the circumstances arose. It would be in his long-term interests to do so.

The floorworkers for the candidates took their places beside the voting line and the poles opened. Media reporters started crowding around Wagner's box. His wife and children sat quietly beside him. The tension was not relieved despite good reports from the floorworkers on the number of Wagner badges going through the lines. There were estimates as high as thirty per cent. On the television set in Wagner's box I heard George Hees assuring Canada that if Wagner had the rumoured 650 votes there would be no stopping him. "People love a winner," George declared, "and they want to be able to say, 'I voted for the winner.'"

During the long wait for the official announcement Paul Hellyer phoned Wagner in his box. Acknowledging that he was doing poorly, he said he would be coming down to support Wagner and wanted to work with him. Wagner thanked him.

At last came the announcement in alphabetical order. Clark, 277. Instantly there was a great roar in the stands. That vote made him a major contender.

Fraser, 127. Gillies, 87. Grafftey, 33. The crowd, remembering his fiery oratory twenty-four hours earlier, gave him an ovation.

Hellyer, 231. That meant he was out. Horner, 235. Ahead of Hellyer. Horner's got more strength in the country than he was ever credited with.

Flora MacDonald, 214. Way below Clark. What happened? No time to figure it out.

Mulroney, 357. Is that good or bad? He probably can't take off on that figure but he's likely to cut into Wagner's initial strength. Nowlan, 86. Stevens, 182. That's a surprise. Almost a hundred below Clark.

Wagner, 531. His supporters cheered because he was well out in first place. But it's not enough. Unless he could jump fast on the second ballot he might not make it. That meant a quick movement to him by Hellyer and Stevens.

The winner could now at least be identified as one of the top three: Wagner, Mulroney or Clark. Mulroney would simply not be accepted. My dreaded scenario was looming ahead.

I looked around for Hellyer but there was no sign of him. Runners were dispatched to his box to tell him to hurry up and file his withdrawal before the fifteen-minute deadline expired. The phone in the box rang. "Stevens is going to Clark." "You mean Wagner," I said. "No, it's Clark." A dark frown covered Wagner's face. Opposing Mulroney and forced to choose between Wagner and Clark, Stevens figured Clark's organizational ability and fresh image would help the Party; ideological closeness to Wagner was overshadowed in Stevens' mind by Claude's poor campaign. Stevens is a pragmatic man. Clark had the look of the winner about him and demonstrated his acceptability to the centre of the Party. Stevens would make him the winner. And he would do it now, rather than waiting.

Hellyer dallied and the voting began again with his name still on the ballot. But he was out nonetheless and he and his wife came to Wagner's box. The television audience saw what was happening but the delegates were in confusion. Over in the Clark box, Fraser, Gillies and Grafftey were being welcomed. Fraser especially had been influenced by the Stevens' decision. On the television I heard Clark saying, "Stevens is a great parliamentarian and I'm delighted to have him with me."

Microphones were being thrust into the Wagner box. But there was nothing for him to say and we tried to keep the media back. Besides, we felt like caged animals surrounded by hunters. Finally the results of the second ballot were announced.

Clark, 532. Almost a doubling. That's the momentum a winner needs.

Fraser, still on the ballot, but out, 34. Hellyer, also still on the ballot, 118. Damn it. Those are Wagner votes and he needs them now.

Horner, 286. Not much gain. He can't win, but will he get out now? MacDonald, 239. The final blow to a great populist campaign. She'll go instantly to Clark and her supporters are so loyal they'll go with her en masse.

Mulroney, 419. No movement. Now his supporters will have to decide on an alternate. Will enough of his Quebec support move to Wagner? The youth delegates are certain to go to Clark. Nowlan, 42.

Wagner, 667. Not enough. Everybody knows he should be over 800 on the second ballot. The Stevens move was fatal. Well, maybe not. Beside us a great struggle was taking place in the Horner box. His close caucus friends, Bill Skoreyko, Stan Schumacher and Pat Nowlan were pleading with him to move to Wagner immediately. Horner, fury written all over his face, seemed ready to explode. The media crushed into his box like vultures attacking their prey. The Horner people could not even talk with one another. Horner lashed out at a microphone and the reporter went reeling. Wagner watched the scene intently. He needed Horner now but Horner is a proud man and might wait to be knocked off.

"East and West," Wagner's supporters began chanting, "East and West."

"Jack's coming over," someone shouted. Wagner moved out to the aisle to receive him. The two men shook hands. Horner could not speak but his act spoke for him. He had come to a French Canadian on the right thereby proving to the country that politics, not racism, motivates Jack Horner. Wagner felt he should reciprocate. A quick trip to Diefenbaker's box in the centre of the arena seemed appropriate. I thought the handshake conveyed the idea of Wagner himself being a bridge for national unity, but again the effect was probably better on T.V. viewers than on the delegates who could not follow everything going on.

The third ballot results were on the T.V. monitor long before they were announced to the crowd. Clark, 969. Again, almost a doubling. Mulroney, 369. A fallback. And now he was forced off the ballot. Would he declare?

Wagner, 1,003. A good gain but this was the ballot that was to put him over. The winner needed 1,171. If Wagner and Clark split evenly Mulroney's 369 votes, Wagner would win by 34 votes. But I sensed that Clark would do better on the split. Mulroney's box became bedlam. He would not declare. More Mulroney delegates could be seen going to Clark than coming to Wagner. Diefenbaker, his path lit by television cameras, came to bestow his blessing on Wagner. But the delegates knew they had the power, not the bosses. The young delegates could not identify with Wagner. They could with Clark.

The voting was called. Wagner returned to his box after voting and sat serenely. The media hovered. Through the maze of people I could see Eva and our daughter Evita sitting in the corner stands. I smiled at them and shrugged my shoulders to tell them that I just could not predict the winner. But inside me I felt it was over. The candidates, except Wagner and Clark, were called to the stage. Horner stopped to shake hands with Wagner and told him he had just heard on the phone that it was Clark.

Ten more minutes of waiting. Then the announcement.

Clark, 1,187

Wagner, 1,122

Sixty-five votes. Thirty-three people.

Wagner kissed his wife. The M.P.s around him again escorted him to the stage. "Yesterday," he told the hushed crowd, "I said we would be writing a page of Canadian history. Today I have the impression that we have written a book." The crowd broke into applause, relieved that he was taking the loss in good spirit. His speech was so good that Dalton Camp was moved to write: "In the context of the Tory Party's history and in the sense of the moment, it had a grace and eloquence that, in the annals of second-place finishers in such contests, is very likely the best ever heard."

Clark came forward, a bright yellow daffodil pinned to his jacket. His wife Maureen, displaying the yellow Clark scarf, stood with him as the crowd gave him the first hurrah as leader. He described the other candidates as his friends. And they would work together to win the country "not by storm or stealth or surprise but by hard work." He struck the note of his own campaign: "The voters don't want to know what we're against, they want to know what we're for."

When it was over Wagner eased back to his family and a tearful embrace. Then they left by a back door for the privacy of their home. I turned back to find Eva and Evita and bumped into Claude Ryan, editor of *Le Devoir*. Why he had given the support of his prestigious French journal to Mulroney was a mystery to me but I didn't feel like arguing. "I just hope, Claude, that you will tell your readers tomorrow that the Conservative Party did not reject a French Canadian," I told him. "You know and I know that there was a cross-current of reasons why Wagner lost. The fund hurt Wagner. So did his image at the end compared to the freshness of Clark. Yes, some people wouldn't vote for a French Canadian but Clark had some Quebecers and Wagner had some westerners. The stop-Wagner movement had a mixture of reasons within it, including a left-right split in the Party. English Canada didn't gang up on Wagner—he ended up with far more votes than there were Quebec delegates. And when you insert into this hodgepodge the strange crossover of Sinclair Stevens, it's impossible to say what, specifically, brought Wagner down. He didn't have enough opening strength in Quebec. Suppose Hellyer had got out as fast as Stevens had? No, Claude, tell your readers that any one of all these factors could have made the difference of thirty-three people."

"How about your writing this for *Le Devoir*?" Ryan asked me.

"I'm too tired, Claude," I answered. "You write it."

I gathered up Eva and Evita and headed outside. Not a taxi. So we took a bus downtown. Standing next to me was our friend, Gerry Amerongen, Speaker of the Alberta legislature. "In politics," Gerry said as we bounced along Ottawa's snow-covered streets, "winning is its own reward. Fortunately for most of us, there is another reward coming that depends on one's effort here below."

In our apartment I sank into a hot bath. My body was aching and I didn't want to go anywhere or do anything for a week. Eva brought me a drink and sat down because she knew I wanted to talk.

I told her that her political judgment was pretty good. She had backed Clark months earlier. In turn she told me that she had developed a warm and favourable feeling for Wagner during the convention. I said I suspected that happened to a lot of people. We were trying to come together. The campaign, producing different viewpoints between us, had been a strain on us personally.

"Well," I laughed, "how would you like to be an Alberta M.P.

who really likes Joe Clark but who worked not once but twice against him? I pushed both Lougheed and Wagner. It would be better for my career to be an Alberta opponent that he now needed to support him than an Alberta friend whom he doesn't need."

"Don't sell yourself so short," Eva said. "And since when did you start thinking politics was going to be your whole life?" She went out to the kitchen to get some food and I sank back in the tub in a state of bewilderment, knowing, finally, just how tough politics is.

LEARNING ABOUT LIFE FROM MICKEY

The picture shows Mickey sitting up holding a rubber ball. Her face is chubby, almost smiling, and her two pony tails give her a saucy look. She is beautiful. Of course, I may not be entirely objective. Mickey is our daughter, the third of six children born to Eva and me.

When the picture was taken Mickey was almost two. There were no real signs of what was ahead. It was only gradually that we noticed she did not relate to people. She could walk and she was happy. But she could not feed herself and she never uttered a word. She didn't seem to hear us. She was in her own little world. The more she grew physically, the more she resisted responding to anything beyond the range of a baby. The doctors were wary of making a definitive analysis and she was subjected to innumerable tests. Inevitably, the decision came. Mickey was mentally retarded. Her brain was congenitally damaged. She had motor problems. She would never be able to take on the normal functions of a growing person.

Through these early years nothing seemed perfectly clear. I learned that eighty-five per cent of mentally retarded people are educable so that they can in varying degrees participate in community life. Another thirteen per cent are trainable whereby they can basically take care of themselves but will always have to live in a sheltered environment, whether a workshop or nursing home. The final two percent, needing total personal care, are custodial. Mickey belonged in the last category. Even this realization was blunted by hope. Maybe an operation, maybe a new discovery—something might happen to allow her at least some mental development.

When she was about seven or eight she seemed to peak. She was still walking, though gradually her feet were beginning to turn inward. She would walk around the house or the backyard with her hand in her mouth, oblivious to the other children playing. But her physical condition began to deteriorate. She had to spend more time seated; handling her became more awkward. Specialists felt she also had multiple sclerosis, causing jerky, unstable physical movements. We took her to the Institute for Human Potential in Philadelphia. We inaugurated patterning exercises, requiring teams of volunteer neighbours to come in every hour to massage and stretch her limbs. Eva took her to Lourdes on a pilgrimage of the sick. Out of all this we still had Mickey, who could smile at us, occasionally laugh out loud at some amusement known only to herself, and cry when she had a pain or was hungry or thirsty.

Eva and I never liked people commiserating with us about this "blow" to our lives. To begin with it was all so gradual that we just accepted each new bit of information, allowing the total picture to come into focus slowly. It was hard for Eva—the physical care, the strain, the fears—but she won't like my saying this publicly. It was Eva's strength that enabled Mickey to feel the family warmth around her. We worried that the other children would somehow be deprived because of the special care and constant supervision Mickey required. This concern, however, made us compensate to the others with special attention. What parent can ever figure all this out? Each child is so special.

Anyway it seemed to us that no one was being hurt by Mickey (she was extremely placid, just the reverse of some retarded children) and that actually the other children were learning something of the quality of compassion. When we drove across the United States on our way to our new home in Edmonton, Mickey came with us, with Eva's mother as her special companion. As we say when we look at our home movies, the children swam their way across the continent, one motel pool after another. We had a great time—and there have been lots of great times, as well as a few tears.

Mickey came into her teen years. A little regression. A plateau. A little regression. We could see the day coming when it would be clear that a hospital could take care of Mickey better than we could.

The decision was made in 1970 and Mickey entered St. Joseph's Hospital, a couple of miles from our home. That was not a happy day. But we know that she gets excellent care and we visit her often. She is as happy as it is possible for her to be.

Now she is twenty. As I look at her in her hospital bed I realize that Mickey has taught me more about life than any book or any other person. If I now have strong feelings about the assault on life that is a chief characteristic of modern society, Mickey is in many ways responsible. I do not put forward the right to life case on intellectual grounds only. My approach is conditioned by my experience with Mickey as a severely handicapped but no less human person. I believe in Mickey's rights as well as those of my other children.

Mickey's rights are under attack by what I call the "convenience philosophy." This philosophy has many adherents, famous and anonymous, and it takes many forms. It demands a response from legislators because it cuts to the basic questions of the right to life. It is a public question affecting the common good and it demands a public response.

In this book I am trying to put forward the need for a public philosophy based on universal values that have their roots in the dignity of the human person. It is essential that this inquiry into values, as an essential part of the political vocation, extend into the basic questions of life and death. I stress this because of the desensitization of our society to all forms of violence—not just in the streets but in our private and collective lives—in the world condition, in entertainment, literature, the arts. The violence and brutality that assaults us in our daily watching of T.V. reflects the decline in respect for the integrity of life itself.

It is asking too much of the politician to hold him responsible for the desensitivity toward life but it is not asking too much to have him consider the basic nature of man. This, in fact, is history's most recurrent debate. But it now has a new urgency because of scientific developments, unsuspected a generation ago, that enable us to choose life or death. These developments are hastening the erosion of a traditional ethic which placed great emphasis on the intrinsic worth and equal value of every human life regardless of its stage or condition; and substituting a new ethic based on utilitarianism.

Deep problems of public morality have been opened up by the scientists. It is not only theologians and behaviourists who must respond but also those who make the laws that will themselves reflect the prevailing values. The question is not whether values are going to determine the implementation of scientific development but which values—or whose values. We point to nuclear weapons as an example of the failure of values to prevail over technology. It is no such thing. What it proves, on the contrary is that the values of fear, defensiveness and threat are still the dominant values of men in the era of nation-states. It is not that science controls values but that, too often, the wrong values control science.

We now have biochemical knowledge about the human mind and new drugs and techniques for producing profound changes in the human personality. Psychologists and behaviourists are leading us into a world in which human beings can be moulded, manipulated and virtually programmed to produce a computerized result. The skills of basic medicine itself are now so sophisticated that talk of "putting together" a human being using the parts of others is not science fiction.

The results are marvellous: children with physical defects are now saved from what formerly would have been certain death.

The results are baffling: the aging clocks in the body will be able to be controlled, adding many years to longevity and thereby changing the complexion of society.

The results are evil: the desire for human perfection has produced a mentality that would do away with life that cannot measure up to arbitrary standards.

In short, medicine and science have raced into the age of discontinuity. Ethics and the law straggle behind. Nothing is clear. We spend millions on medical research to cure fatal diseases and pass laws that permit the destruction of unborn children. We go to extraordinary lengths to keep alive by machines elderly people in the natural process of dying and accept the deliberate injection of poison into a terminally ill patient to end the suffering immediately. It is no wonder that a capital punishment debate becomes lost in emotions. We feel strongly about life and death—but we do not know what we feel. Even the standards of who is alive (the fetus) and who is dead (the heart transplant patient) are uncertain. It is not just the meaning and direction of life in the modern world that are confused. It is the value of life itself.

In my mind these discordancies are directly connected to the mental outlook produced by the industrial civilization with its incessant demand for production. If we do not produce, we have no value. That is the philosophy that subsumes every ethical value we try to teach our children. We did not start this. It has been so for generations in the western world. The inherent value of the individual has been superseded by the value placed upon him in terms of his ability to contribute to, or exploit, society.

Our age, with its sudden dynamism and dislocations of familiar patterns, has merely focused a new light on the devaluation of man. At the very time when religion is needed to explain the nature of man and help us establish priorities for his peaceful development in the global community, religion is virtually impotent. Religion for so long has dwelled on the internal spirituality of man and the secular world for so long has treated spirituality perfunctorily, that an erosion of publicly held ethical values has taken place.

Into this void stepped utilitarianism, the only ethic we have to guide us: "If it's got some values that we can see, it must be good." Nowhere is the inversion of human values seen in its most devastating repercussions than in the popular morality advanced by Dr. Joseph Fletcher, one of the fathers of situation ethics. The Fletcher thesis is that "mere biological life . . . is without personal status." He lists the qualities that are the marks of personal being: minimal intelligence (anyone with an IQ below forty is probably not a person), self-awareness, self-control, a sense of time, of futurity and of the past; concern for others, ability to communicate with others, control of existence, curiosity, changeability and creativity, a balance of rationality and feeling, distinctiveness and brain functioning. These criteria of personhood are equated by Fletcher with humanhood. If you do not measure up to Fletcher's minimum standard, you are not human. What then? The Fletcher answer is that society should dispose of elements not measuring up.

Fletcher can sit in his ivory tower and rationalize forever, but that's my daughter he's talking about. To say that Mickey is not human and thereby not deserving of life because she is "substandard" is a monstrous statement. It is not only devoid of compassion, it violates a law of nature by decreeing that some creatures are more worthy of life than others. Where does such an insidious philosophy end? If we keep raising the standards who among us can be guaranteed survival?

At the root of our social and legal system is the shared conviction that each human life has a unique value that cannot be measured. This conviction is embodied in our welfare legislation which strives to ensure that all people, including the poor, the old, the sick, the disabled and the unemployed, can live their lives in comfort and dignity. This conviction is acted upon dramatically in times of emergency or disaster.

Only in the past decade or two has there been a counter-movement against the accepted belief that a human life has a unique value. Those who advocate abortion on demand are prepared to refuse the life of the unborn child legal recognition and to have it disposed of, because it is immature. Their attitude reflects a disturbing hostility and callousness toward the weak and helpless. This mentality does not stop at excluding the unborn from the human family. Increasing numbers are proposing that the senile, the incurably ill and the deformed should be able to be killed with or without their permission.

Millard S. Everett writes in *Ideals of Life*: "When public opinion is prepared for it, no child shall be admitted into the society of the living who would be certain to suffer any social handicap—for example, any physical or mental defect that would prevent marriage or would make others tolerate his company only from a sense of mercy. . . . Life in early infancy is very close to nonexistence, and admitting a child into our society is almost like admitting one from potential to actual existence, and viewed in this way only normal life should be accepted."

Here I think we can see a little bit of future thinking. As infant mortality goes down and disease is further vanquished and population demands on the earth's resources increase, there will be special challenges to the right to life of defective children. It is not alarmist to point out that as soon as society permits one group to be excluded from legal protection, it is on the road to excluding other groups who may be considered "useless," or whose interests may conflict with the dominant social class.

I do not mean to indicate that all medical-moral problems can be slotted into black-and-white formulas. It is precisely because there are so many complex cases coming before us that we must, as a society, agree on a common basis for the right to life in order to properly evaluate each one. What exactly is the legal position of a doctor—and a parent—in deciding what efforts should be made to save a baby born with multiple anomalies (e.g. hydrocephalus, inoperative genito-urinary abnormalities) or major cardio-pulmonary disorders? Should an obviously doomed child be allowed to die by not feeding it?

Dr. Raymond S. Duff of Yale University and Dr. A. G. M. Campbell of the University of Aberdeen, Scotland, published in the *New England Journal of Medicine* the cases of forty-three infants permitted to die because vital treatment was deliberately withheld. One of the babies had an incurable lung disease; he was chronically blue, laboured to breathe, had a weak heart and at five months still needed forty per cent oxygen to survive. His moderate-income parents had already spent $15,000 on his hospital care; the other children in the family had become physically disturbed; the marriage itself was threatened. Finally the decision was made to take the baby off oxygen. He died three hours later. "The nurses, parents and physicians," Duff and Campbell wrote, "all were attached to this child, whose life they had tried so hard to make worthwhile. They considered it cruel to continue, and yet difficult to stop."

In most instances, the two doctors reported, parents of deformed children thought there were limits to what they could or should be expected to bear. Most of them, however, wanted maximum efforts to sustain life and to rehabilitate the handicapped child. In these difficult cases someone, usually the doctor, must decide whether extreme measures should be taken to prolong life or whether to accept the message of nature that this child was meant to live but briefly and allow it to die peacefully. No legislator wants these decisions thrust on him. A just law must provide for individual decision in doubtful cases. But how different this respect for complex cases is from the wholesale condemnation of defective children advanced by Fletcher and Everett.

One of the most moving sights I ever saw on television occurred on Roy Bonisteel's *Man Alive* on the CBC. In a program on measuring humanity Bonisteel allowed Fletcher to give his selection criteria for those who will be allowed to survive; then he switched to an interview with Sondra Diamond, a very seriously deformed woman of thirty-five who spoke with great difficulty. The list of defects in Sondra Diamond's physical condition is a long one. She has, however, an IQ of 140 and by dint of sheer effort has become a psychologist.

This is precisely why surveys of popular morality must never replace the determination of a society to frame its laws on principles. Here the principle is the right to life without a physical or mental test. It is true that the skill, time and money often invested in individual cases of critical deformation are out of proportion to subsequent efforts and expense to help less seriously maimed children attain social adjustment. In spite of this disproportion, I cannot conclude that children with marked deformities should be condemned to death. As Bernard Haring observes in *Medical Ethics*, "Only through faith in the dignity of each person will the medical profession and mature parents find the golden mean."

On the one hand no man has a right to declare another human life meaningless, since man's dignity does not depend on his efficiency or his capacity to contribute to the economy. On the other hand when the life of extremely disabled and abnormal children means no more than a basic existence, they need not, and sometimes should not, be sustained in life by all means available. Medicine alone cannot bear the full burden of responsibility. There needs to be a sincere dialogue with the behavioural sciences, philosophy and theology. A better-informed public opinion on the right-to-life question is essential. Legislators cannot remain aloof. For we need laws which uphold the principle of life and yet are responsive to genuine human dilemma—without opening the door to a flood of abuse, as in abortions.

❧❧❧

The idea that abortion is exclusively a religious issue, let alone a Catholic one, is a myth. A statement signed by the leaders of thirteen Christian churches in Canada emphasized that Canadians, regardless of religious persuasion, must be concerned about the massive and accelerating increase in the number of abortions in Canada: "The irreverence for life demonstrated by the increasingly casual attitudes of some who advocate not just the changing of the law on abortion, but the violation of the laws that exist is, we believe, a threat to all of us; it is the antithesis to our Christian belief that human life is of infinite value."

Whatever one's convictions are about religion, I believe the arguments against abortion as public policy can be cogently stated without resort to religion. And in a secular society it is entirely proper that we argue the abortion question in terms acceptable to all. That is one of the requirements for articulating a public philosophy which will bring our society to a consensus. In fact the book *Abortion and Social Justice* sets out the full range of arguments against abortion —biological, medical, psychological, sociological, legal, demographic and ethical—without a single paper among the nineteen being theological or pragmatically religious.

Abortion is not a private matter. The destruction of human life, even "incipient" or developing human life in the womb, can never be considered a private matter under our law. Would those civil libertarians who argue that abortion is a private matter argue that the exercise of civil rights is purely a private matter between the black man and the man who thwarts them? Certainly not. Just as the civil right to vote must be protected by law, so too must the most fundamental and basic of all civil rights—the right to life.

We must understand that abortion is not merely a sectarian religious problem or one for the area of "private" morality. Abortion is nothing less than a question of civil rights: does the unborn child have a civil right to life? If the child does, is it not then the duty of all citizens, regardless of religious faith or private moral sensitivities, to protect the unborn child's civil rights?

The position that our law takes on abortion indicates the position it will take on euthanasia, genetic engineering, cloning and all of the different human life problems facing our society in the years ahead. Those who argue for the unborn child's right to life are arguing not only for the unborn child but for the civil right to life of every human being including the mentally ill, the aged, the genetically incompetent. If the law abandons the protection of the civil rights of the innocent child in the womb, it will one day abandon its protection of the civil right to life of the mentally incompetent, the senile and the hopelessly ill.

Supporters of abortion often argue that the baby in the womb is not a human but merely a piece of tissue attached to the mother. If there were any scientific doubt of the humanity of the unborn— which there is not—surely the burden of proof would rest with those who would deny the humanity of the unborn. Even if there were doubt, it would have to be acknowledged that the wisest, most prudent policy would be to give the benefit of the doubt to those whose humanity is questioned.

Actually the development of the individual in the womb is extremely rapid. The heart begins beating within twenty-one days of conception; blood vessels and circulating blood, a backbone, skeletal system and brainwaves are traceable by forty-three days; then over the next few weeks rudimentary organs, liver, kidneys and digestive tract, arms and legs, fingers and toes, eyes, ears and a mouth are formed. At the very moment of fertilization all the unique genetic characteristics are determined: eye, skin and hair colouring, height and bone structure, intellectual potential and inherited emotional makeup. From the time of conception forty-six chromosomes are present, twenty-three from each parent. This is the chromosomal development defined by biologists as that of a normal human being. This small individual requires only nutrition and normal conditions in order to develop in the full pattern of human life.

That there is rampant abuse in Canada's abortion law seems to me indisputable. In 1969 the Criminal Code was amended in an

omnibus bill. Section 251 permitted an accredited hospital therapeutic abortion committee to allow an abortion when the continua-
tion of a woman's pregnancy "would be likely to endanger her life
or health." It is very clear from the debates in Parliament and from
the reasons given by the government on introducing the bill that the
new law was meant to be restrictive, to be applied when there were
genuine cases of medical need.

Several Members wanted to qualify the health danger clause by
adding the words "a clear and direct serious threat" as a condition
for doing an abortion. John Turner, then Justice Minister, turned
down the amendment. "Health," he said, "is incapable of definition
and will be left to the good professional judgment of medical prac-
titioners to decide." Others wanted the insertion of a "conscience
clause" stating that no person and no institution could be forced to
perform abortions or aid in performing them. The government rejected this also, arguing that it was self-evident that no one should
be forced to participate. The new law, Turner said, "imposes no
duty on the board of a hospital to set up a therapeutic abortion committee" and "it imposes no duty . . . to perform an abortion." Turner
clearly stated that it was not the intention of the government to have
abortion on demand. He specifically excluded abortion for social
or economic reasons, for rape, or for the risk of deformity of the
fetus.

As an editor I wrote at the time that the government was talking
out of both sides of its mouth and that the new law was so loosely
written that it would open the door to abortion on demand. But in
the climate of 1969, a time of questioning of old values, the abortion
section of the omnibus bill passed easily—especially since the Liberal Whip was used. Despite the wording of the law, however, it was
not the intention of Parliament to throw open the abortion door.

But what happened? In 1970, the year after the new law was
passed, there were 11,152 recorded abortions in Canada. Two years
later the number had jumped to 38,853, a rate of 11.2 abortions per
100 live births. In 1973 there were 43,201 abortions, 12.6 per 100
live births. In 1974 the number went up to 48,136—which was a

rate of 14 abortions per 100 live births. The abortion rate varies widely across Canada. British Columbia had the highest 1974 rate at 29.2 and Newfoundland the lowest at 1.5 per 100 births. The rate in the other provinces: Ontario, 20; Alberta, 15; Manitoba, 8.3; Nova Scotia, 8; Saskatchewan, 7.9; Northwest Territories, 6.2; Quebec, 5.3; New Brunswick, 3.8; Prince Edward Island, 2.6.

In some hospitals the number of abortions now equals or exceeds the number of live births. For example, at Toronto General Hospital, 2,000 babies were delivered in 1973 and 2,900 abortions performed. In 1974 6,275 pregnant women entered Vancouver General Hospital; 2,275 of them had a live baby. This fits into the statistical trends of those countries where abortions are easy to obtain; in New York City the abortion rate is 157.8 per cent of live births. Countries like Bulgaria, Hungary and Japan, which have had freely available abortion for many years, now experience abortion rates ranging from about 40 to 130 for every 100 live births.

It is ludicrous to suggest that the state of health of pregnant women in Canada was five times worse in 1974 than in 1970. Yet there were nearly five times as many abortions. The law, strictly interpreted, permits abortions only when the mother's life or health is endangered. It is straining credibility to suggest that it is more dangerous to be pregnant in the three richest provinces of British Columbia, Ontario and Alberta where the abortion rate is far higher than in any other province. Obviously the interpretation of the word "health" is so wide as to throw the law into disrepute. Abortions are being performed because a growing number of women are deciding that they do not want to carry their child to term. An unwanted pregnancy has been interpreted by many hospital abortion committees as a threat to health. Thus abortion in these hospitals has become a necessary medical service available on demand.

If the hospital committees did more comprehensive work, more women might receive counselling to show them that while the pregnancy may be unwanted, the child is not. The mother may not want to keep the child but adoption agencies now have more requests for children than are available. Much more psychological and social support should be given to pregnant women who do not know what to do. Instead of being steered to abortion they could be helped to understand that there are others who want to adopt.

Because I was becoming increasingly concerned at the flaunting of the law, I gave my support in 1973 to the newly formed Alliance for Life, a citizens' movement, to protest the abortion escalation. A rally, headed by Dr. Heather Morris, a gynaecologist, Malcolm Muggeridge, the British author and pro-life lecturer, and Morris Shumiatcher, author of Canada's first bill of rights in Saskatchewan, was held in Ottawa and an anti-abortion petition bearing 350,000 signatures was presented to the government. A march on Parliament Hill was held and I was asked to join the leaders.

On a bitingly cold November Saturday afternoon 3,500 men and women carrying banners and white flowers marched through the streets and onto the hill where the flowers were placed on the steps of Parliament in memory of the unborn aborted. The occasion brought out a fighting speech from me. "In fighting for the rights of the unborn," I said, "we are fighting for the rights of every person whose life might at some time be taken unjustly—the aged, the defective, the infirm." Then I threw out a challenge: "Go back to your homes across Canada and get one million signatures on another petition. Then let the government dare to say that Canadians want abortion on demand."

Alliance for Life took up the challenge and two weeks later I went to Toronto for a press conference to launch the drive. A rally was held in Edmonton where I told the audience that Canadians must be told that abortion had become a social instead of a medical problem. "In fact," I said, "I now believe abortion to be the most alarming social problem in Canada today."

Several constituents wrote letters to me—and the local paper— criticizing my "distorted" sense of social values. One of my supporters wrote insisting that "abortion is no more an issue for legislation than the religion which I choose to adopt." She is the mother of four children and says she would not hesitate to seek an abortion if she desired one: "I believe that I have the legal right to hold and to practise my opinion without interference from the government in this matter."

This became a prevalent view. Another of my constituents, a man, wrote protesting that my "outraged moralism" was blinding me to a "sensitive and compassionate analysis" that would lead me to take abortion out of the Criminal Code: "I urge you to show those of us who are deeply interested what you are *for*; do not merely become one of those indignant know-nothings who is against permissiveness, immorality, etc. etc."

Mail started coming from across the country and since then has run second only to capital punishment in steady volume. Since I was identified so strongly as an anti-abortionist, many people with similar feelings wrote to support me. I have never been able to use the mail, therefore, as an accurate barometer of public opinion. But I have gained the impression that the attitude of many is pulling back from any further loosening of the present law. This is happening despite the biased pro-abortion attitude of the national media and the sympathy directed to Dr. Henry Morgentaler, a crusading abortionist. The Morgentaler case has excited further reaction because a jury first acquitted him of performing an illegal abortion only to have the verdict reversed by an appeal court. Parliament has since changed the Criminal Code so that a jury acquittal cannot be reversed; an appeal court may, however, order a new trial.

The publicity surrounding the Alliance for Life activities began to change the attitudes of several Members of Parliament who became concerned at the rapidly growing number of abortions. After the 1974 election an all-party Parliamentary Group in Defence of the Unborn was formed with Ursula Appolloni, a Liberal and one of the few women M.P.s opposed to abortion, as chairman and Dr. Bob Holmes, a Conservative and medical practitioner, as vice-chairman. We presented a statement, signed by eighty-three M.P.s, to the government demanding legislation "to restrict abortions to cases where the medical need is indisputable."

This put the government squarely in the middle of mounting pressure from both sides of the abortion question. The federal Advisory Council on the Status of Women and provincial councils in Ontario, Quebec and Saskatchewan all declared that a woman should have the right to decide if she will terminate her own pregnancy. The

Alliance for Life presented a brief to the Prime Minister demanding "amendments to the law which will guarantee equal protection to the child conceived but not yet born."

The development of the Petition of One Million proved to be a gigantic logistical job for a volunteer organization but over the months about ninety anti-abortion groups sprang up across the country. And on May 29, 1975 some 500 of their leaders converged on Parliament Hill with thirty-five cases containing 1,027,425 signatures to the petition which said simply: "Over one million Canadians call upon Parliament to enact legislation providing for the child conceived but not yet born the same protection as is provided for any other person, and also urge Parliament to show leadership in fostering a life-sustaining society."

Altogether a crowd of 3,000 persons assembled beneath the Peace Tower to demonstrate their concern. Ten Members of Parliament from each of the provinces* formally received the petition. The packing cases were left in the lobby as the House opened at 2 p.m. with a barrage of questions to Justice Minister Otto Lang. Stanfield asked if any proposed abortion inquiry would deal with the quality of the present legislation or merely its administration. All Lang would say was that the issue would be studied "with great thoroughness."

The pro-life delegates had jammed the galleries and I made an oblique reference to them as I rose to put forth my question: "My supplementary arises from the fact that the largest petition ever brought into Parliament was presented today, signed by one million Canadians from the Atlantic to the Pacific, and asking for much faster action than the Minister of Justice seems to imply will be forthcoming." At this point the galleries applauded loudly—which is not allowed—joining desk-pounding by M.P.s who revealed a pro-life mood in the House as I had never before seen it: "I should like

---

*Angus MacLean, P.C., Prince Edward Island; James McGrath, P.C., Newfoundland; Andy Hogan, N.D.P., Nova Scotia; Maurice Dionne, Lib., New Brunswick; André Fortin, S.C., Quebec; Ursula Appolloni, Lib., Ontario; Walter Dinsdale, P.C., Manitoba; Cliff McIsaac, Lib., Saskatchewan; Douglas Roche, P.C., Alberta; Bob Briscoe, P.C., British Columbia.

to ask the Minister, as he considers what kind of examination this question will be given and when, whether he would specifically consider the empowering of a committee to be set up to subpoena the records of hospital abortion committees to see whether cases are found in which abortions were permitted when the life or health of the mother was not in danger and if so, whether charges will be laid and by whom?"

"Mr. Speaker," Lang responded, "the power to examine how hospital committees operate was in fact put into the Criminal Code and entrusted to the hands of the provincial ministers of health in the various provinces. I am impressed that many persons who appear to applaud the last question, and might applaud any other question if they thought it appropriate to do so on a given day, apparently have not been pressing their provincial colleagues to take some action in this regard."

This answer reflected an argument that Lang had been advancing for some time, namely that the present law is all right; the fault is in the administration of it which is a provincial matter.

The visitors filed away, drifting down Parliament Hill, most of them not realizing that abortion would be debated during Private Member's Hour when Stuart Leggatt introduced a motion calling on the government to produce correspondence between the Minister of Justice and the provinces on the abortion question. The motion had been sitting since the previous fall and Leggatt chose this day to advance it to enable him to make a pro-abortion speech and defend Dr. Morgentaler. Ursula Appolloni, Holmes and I made pro-life speeches but the numbers in the House were too small to get a reading on the mood and, of course, there was no vote.

That evening the House returned to debating an omnibus bill on women's rights that was the government's bow to International Women's Year. Not many Members were entering the debate but I thought I should express concern for the total picture of women's rights and their role in society to complement my views on abortion. In other words, I am not just against abortion; I am for measures to enable women's rights to be advanced as part of the whole human rights field. Despite the fanfare of International Women's Year, most women still find themselves working in clerical and service jobs at low pay. They are still discriminated against in employment and housing. They still make up the majority of social assistance recipients. There is still inadequate daycare. In Canada today there are more than 300,000 one-parent families (ten per cent of all families) and a disproportionate number are headed by women who have extreme financial difficulties and interrelated serious social problems. There was barely a quorum in the House, not even the women M.P.s seemed enthusiastic, and the debate fizzled out.

In our convoluted parliamentary system not even a petition of one million Canadians is enough to ensure action. The next day in the House I argued that a petition of such magnitude ought at least to be debated but the Speaker ruled out a debate because "it is the Members of this House who should make representations respecting changes in the law, and not outsiders by way of petitions." The petition went to the storeroom and the matter was put back into the hands of the government.

A few months later, just before transferring to another portfolio, Lang set up an Abortion Law Study Committee "to determine whether the procedure provided in the Criminal Code for obtaining therapeutic abortions is operating equitably across Canada." In other words, the Committee was to examine the administration rather than the underlying policy. It was a foregone conclusion that the Committee would find inequitable administration since only 258 of Canada's 783 hospitals have abortion committees. A new group called Doctors for Repeal of the Abortion Law was already arguing that "the law discriminates against large numbers of Canadian women by placing safe, legal abortion out of their reach." The poor do not have the same access as the rich, the group said.

If the government had wanted a thorough and complete report on the workings of the present law, it would have examined the abuses of the law. But because abortion in just a few years has become a norm, the government concerned itself only with the availability of the procedure. This is clearly a step toward removal of abortion from the Criminal Code. "It is evident," said Gwen Landolt, president of Alliance for Life, "that the purpose of this fact-finding committee is to rationalize and justify a decision to widen the abortion law."

Frequent and substantial changes in abortion legislation have been made in recent years in many countries, generally in the direction of making abortions easier to obtain. Several countries, however, such as Romania, Bulgaria, Czechoslovakia and Hungary, after adopting very permissive abortion legislation, have subsequently modified certain provisions and made their legislation more restrictive. Other countries are also in the process of doing so. Permissive abortion has produced a wave of protest in Britain and the U.S.

All of these changes are merely a continuing, fruitless search for the nonexistent "ideal abortion law" and represent a failure to effectively treat the underlying social pathology. Neither allowing abortion nor prohibiting it has done anything to correct the underlying social and economic conditions which cause women to seek abortions. In the long run only by confronting and solving these problems are we likely to find an exit from what has been termed "the abortion dilemma."

As the abortion rate escalates, abortion becomes more socially acceptable and even accepted. Thus an operation legalized because there are genuine cases of conflict of rights between an unborn child and its seriously ill mother has been seized upon by popular morality for social advancement. And the more widespread the practice becomes, the more tolerant society becomes. This is a clear reflection of the lack of public commitment to human life as the highest priority.

The argument that easily available legal abortions will reduce the number of illegal abortions is spurious. An American study of eleven countries which widened their abortion laws reveals that none of the countries experienced a subsequent decline in the criminal abortion rate. Why does the illegal abortion rate not decline? The Alliance for Life brief to the government suggested that there are always some people for whom the legal procedures are not speedy or secret enough.

I have often wished that doctors would raise their voices against abortion. Their status in society is so high that no legislative body— and certainly not the Canadian parliament in 1969—would ignore their demand for tightly controlled abortion laws. But the proponents of wider abortion laws have found allies in many physicians.

Lately, however, I have seen some soul-searching by doctors re-examining the efficacy of abortion. Dr. Bernard Nathanson, once a prominent advocate of abortion on demand, described in *Good Housekeeping* (March, 1976) how, as a director of the busiest licensed abortion facility in the western world, he witnessed the gradual psychological disintegration of many of his staff. A growing number of nurses are revolted at having to gather the fetal parts after they have been dismembered in a suction abortion, dispose of a live fetus after a hysterotomy and deliver a dead child after a saline abortion.

My critics on this subject express the wish that I would speak as strongly in favour of sex education programs in schools and better contraceptive programs for family planning. I do. I support this positive approach provided it is done in an atmosphere that promotes sexual responsibility. It is irresponsible to teach that abortion is the last resort of contraception yet that is precisely what is done by many family and sex counsellors. The federal government itself does this. A set of six booklets, entitled "Sex Education," published by the Family Planning Division of the Department of National Health and Welfare, lumps abortion in with contraceptives as another form of birth control. The great distinction between contraception and abortion is again blurred in an abortion climate. Abortion is not just a "post-contraceptive." Moreover, the easier it is to obtain an abortion, the more lax people become about taking steps to prevent an unwanted pregnancy. A Canadian study by the Abortion, Contraception Counselling and Research Association revealed that sixty per cent of women seeking abortion counselling took no steps to prevent pregnancy, even though they knew about contraception.

What should now be done? The answer is found by going back to the Canadian Bill of Rights (1960) wherein is found: "In Canada there have existed and shall continue to exist without discrimination by reason of race, national origin, colour, religion or sex, the following human rights and fundamental freedoms, namely, a) the right of the individual to life. . . . Moreover, there shall be no "cruel and unusual treatment or punishment" and no person shall be denied his rights without "a fair hearing."

On the question of who is a person, the World Health Organization of the United Nations in 1948 urged respect for human life "from the moment of conception on." In 1959 the U.N. adopted the Declaration of the Rights of the Child based on this preamble: "Whereas the child, by reason of his physical and mental immaturity needs special safeguards and care, including appropriate legal protection, *before as well as after birth.* . . ."

Either we are serious about those declarations or we are not. In my mind Section 251 of the Criminal Code is simply incompatible with the Canadian Bill of Rights. At the very least it should be amended to insist that medical proof be established that the mother's life be *seriously* endangered before permission for abortion is given. When a therapeutic abortion committee considers an application for abortion there should be a legally appointed guardian present to represent the rights of the unborn child. By instituting due process the decision would not be left to doctors alone. In addition, the decisions of the abortion committee should be subject to federal review.

Abortion is a vast subject but I rest my case on these legal considerations. In our time we are concerned with the securing of individual liberties and women's rights. As Professor George H. Williams of Harvard University points out, "We dare not extend them at the expense of the unborn, who need only time to become one with us."

❧

The subject of euthanasia, while not yet discussed as intensively as abortion, is an emotional and ethical issue equally deserving of the closest attention of politicians. Euthanasia comes from the Greek *eu* and *thantos*, meaning a good or peaceful death. It suggests a dignified ending to suffering and hence is often called "death with dignity." The movement to legalize euthanasia is growing; several cases of relatives acceding to the importuning of loved ones who want to be spared an agonizing illness have caught the headlines.

Euthanasia has two aspects, active and passive. "Active" euthanasia means taking a deliberate step to end a person's life for humanitarian purposes. It is "mercy killing"—and it is illegal. "Passive" euthanasia means deliberately choosing not to take mechanical measures to prolong life when death is imminent. In my view, this is permissable since neither patient nor physician should be under any obligation to take extraordinary steps to prolong artificially a life that is in the natural process of ending.

On the surface the distinction between active and passive euthanasia may seem clear but the ramifications are complex. Doctors are faced with terrifying moral decisions about whether to extend the use of extraordinary life-saving devices in hopeless cases, give an overdose of a drug which may relieve pain but is also lethal, or do nothing. There is a myriad of alternatives. These very decisions of doctors are an exercise in passive or active euthanasia and the situation is exacerbated by the different definitions of death now being offered by science. Only rarely are doctors charged with mercy killing; prosecutors and juries are reluctant to question the good faith of doctors or to demand precise proof of whether death was hastened, induced or merely not actively prevented. Still the medical profession rightly fears malpractice suits. This problem was at the heart of the famous Karen Quinlan case in the U.S.

Most doctors endorse the principle of death with dignity, which would give them the option to treat or not to treat an incurably ill patient. At the same time they are generally opposed to the legalizing of active euthanasia, although there is a growing body of medical opinion favouring active euthanasia in certain cases. None of this is simple. Even what appears to be the negative act of *omitting* a special treatment (passive euthanasia) is interpreted by some as an act of *commission*.

Public opinion, meanwhile, is growing in favour of a doctor being allowed deliberately to end the life of an incurably ill and suffering person provided the person and his family request such action. Which leads the euthanasia movement to step up its campaign to demand that "our laws be brought in line with public opinion." Bills permitting death with dignity are now coming before state legislators in the U.S. The effect of these bills would be to make binding what is called "a living will." In this document a person gives direction to his doctor, lawyer and closest relative "to assure that certain measures be taken to end my life" in case of irreparable deterioration of mind or body without realistic hope for recovery.

What is the correct response of society to euthanasia now that politicians are being asked to bring the law up to date with modern developments? Here again a public philosophy establishes principles. If we are concerned with the right to life in the abortion issue, we are here concerned with the right to die. The mere existence of medical machinery does not mean that it must be used in every conceivable case or even that it should be. We cannot deny the inexorable law that death will come to every person. Each one has the right to die with dignity and grace. We see this problem in an anguished way if resuscitation is attempted when it is most probable that the major cortical centres are irreparably damaged or destroyed. The question is: should such a person be artificially kept "alive" for months or years in a fully unconscious state or in one of obvious mental absence or grave disturbance? I do not think that such life should be prolonged artificially when, in particular situations, this means only prolonging suffering and delaying the act of death.

A compelling illustration of the acceptability of passive euthanasia is seen in the case of a terminal cancer patient in Calgary who told a public seminar on the Right to Die that terminal patients should be permitted to decide when treatment should be discontinued. "When there is no more that can be done for me, I should like treatment to be discontinued and the disease to take its course naturally," the patient said from his hospital bed which had been wheeled to the front of the seminar auditorium. That night the patient, a forty-eight-year-old father of five children, took a turn for the worse. Asked if he wanted another operation to remove the fluid from his chest, he consulted with his wife and then declined. He died thirty minutes later.

A guideline, therefore, is that medical progress must not deny a person his right to die with human dignity. How then can the law respond to the ethical question: is the premeditated omission of treatment with the direct intention not to prolong the process of dying permissible? Speaking as one politician, I am not ready to give a definitive answer. This is not to sidestep the issue but only to state that it is so complicated that it demands deep consideration by all who are responsible for ethical leadership in our society.

What *is* certain in my mind is that the correct answer to the problem cannot be offered by those whose basic philosophy of human-hood is utilitarian. To distort passive euthanasia into an unostentatious way to eliminate those whose death is not imminent, but who most probably would have a long, sickly life or never be economically productive would be to falsify the protestation of death with dignity.

As we consider active euthanasia I do not see how a society could accept it. In the protection of the common good the law must be explicit in its prohibition of mercy killing even for well-intentioned humanitarian motives. To give somebody—anybody—direct power to end another's life is to intervene in the life-death process that has its origin outside man himself. Moreover, giving somebody the right to put another to death suggests the *duty* to kill when the reason seems right. Who, even the best intentioned, can find the right criteria for such an unalterable act? The persons "mercifully" to be killed might well, because of their condition, be unfit to make a rational decision based on unwavering conviction. Undoubtedly the legislation of euthanasia would remind the invalid of his newly acquired powers over his own disposal. Is a sense of guilt at being alive to be added to a feeling of resignation—let alone regret—at dying?

I am not dissuaded from my stand against active euthanasia by the argument that death is a private matter between patient and doctor any more than I am convinced that abortion is a private matter. The individual does not protect his own rights; it is society that protects them. Society must have a standard to follow. The result of allowing abortions for what were meant to be serious (and thus exceptional) medical reasons became a travesty of justice. Abortions for social reasons became common once the wedge in the law appeared. Similarly, legalized euthanasia would soon be interpreted as adding to the quality of life in general, although I think the quality of life of our entire society would be poisoned through this kind of nourishment.

It may seem a long step from legally permitting people to request that their own lives be ended, through active euthanasia to a public policy requiring all lives to be terminated according to some external criteria. But escalating bureaucratic control of our lives now gives me no hope that what starts as permission would not be made mandatory by a utilitarian philosophy in an age of machines.

⟶ ❦ ⟵

When we turn to the coming era of biogenetic engineering the issues of abortion and euthanasia seem like kindergarten. The ethical problems that legislators will have to face in the years ahead would baffle Socrates. For genetic knowledge and techniques of genetic control will make it possible to create new versions of man. For the first time in history man will have the potential to improve the conditions of the entire human race or destroy it by taking over deliberate control of his own evolution. As J.-G. Castel, editor of the *Canadian Bar Review*, pictures it in an article called "Legal Implications of Biomedical Science and Technology in the 21st Century," we may be reading this kind of advertisement by the year 2000:

> Buy a human egg, rent a womb, shop for a super baby, grow a new heart, wake up in the year 3000.

Scientific research, Castel points out, "raises ethical, moral, legal, and political questions as a conflict often exists between the rights of the individual and the good of society." For instance, what is or is not legitimate in human experimentation?

Scientists envisage babies being created by the artificial mixing of sperm and ovum and the entire gestation process carried on outside the mother's body. Who will raise test-tube babies? Who are the parents when a natural ovum or sperm have not been used? "Until now we could have sex without babies, in the future we will be able to have babies without sex," says Castel. "Can reproduction be depersonalized without people becoming dehumanized?"

When to all this is added the possibility of reproducing complete duplicates of people through the process of cloning, the future promises marvels or disaster, depending on your viewpoint. Much of the human organism will likely be replaceable. The imagination of lawyers and judges, not to mention politicians, will surely be taxed by questions like these: What is the status of a person who has his brain transplanted into a new body grown by clonal reproduction of himself? Should a man be permitted to have his brain transplanted into a female body?

Genetic and behavioural control will raise stupendous questions concerning the nature of individual freedom and the civil rights issue of invasion of privacy. A breakthrough into a higher level of humanhood or dehumanization? Which will it be?

How will we ever be able even to approach these questions without a commonly accepted principle concerning the fundamental dignity of human life? Once again we see the need for public discourse concerning the principles of human life as we understand it today. For tomorrow the genetic discoveries will be too much for us to handle without a firm understanding of humanhood.

It is true that many scientists—sociologists, anthropologists and psychologists among them—are questioning the vision of a utopia engineered by human minds. Dr. Rollo May, perhaps the world's leading humanistic psychoanalyst, warns that the behaviourists must beware lest they create a totally mechanical society. "My hope is that the human being will be rediscovered," he says. With this rediscovery, he hopes, will come a new emphasis on love, creativity, music and all the other qualitative, introspective experiences. Viennese psychiatrist Viktor Frankl, in his own field, complements May by seeking to free man's spiritual unconsciousness so that he can realize his innate need to find meaning in his life. For to ignore his concern with values is to fail to do justice to "the humanness of man."

As the politician begins to consider his own role in a future that man will create he cannot escape his obligation to follow principles that will protect human rights and human freedom. The vocabulary of politics will thus have to deepen. Without expunging our own backgrounds, we must come together in a sincere desire to find the laws that will express a public philosophy. No one of us in Parliament has all the answers to these difficult questions of life and death. But I have a trust in the common wisdom that is bound to emerge in discussions and debates shorn of political posturing and partisanship.

Some of my colleagues dispute the idea that Members of Parliament should be ethical leaders. Mark MacGuigan, a noted civil libertarian and law professor who has served in Parliament since 1968, discussed this one day with me. "Parliament," he said, "is a pragmatic institution and we're elected to do a certain limited job, to make decisions in the areas in which people expect we will. We can easily take undue advantage of our position to try to parade our own values across the public scene. To my mind we need to exercise a certain amount of self-restraint as parliamentarians. Although abortion is a matter of public morality, I must admit that I think the politician should treat it as a matter of private morality in giving leadership in that area."

"But it's precisely because the questions of our society have to do with ethics that we cannot abstain from ethical leadership," I answered. "We can increase the consciousness of ethical leadership not in the sense of a bishop preaching to his people but as legislators agreeing on a basic value system. We do this by concentrating on a public philosophy, which is the recognition of immutable laws to which all men of goodwill can subscribe."

MacGuigan responded, "We over-estimate ourselves if we think of ourselves as ethically equipped. I think a politician has the duty to state clearly his position on the life and death issues to his voters, and I have tried to do that. But I don't think that he has the duty to proselytize for his values as, for example, I would proselytize for equality of opportunity. In the very divided state of opinion in our society, I just don't think this is an appropriate matter on which a politician can give leadership. There are many other agencies which can give leadership. The great failing here is in the churches. I don't think a politician can make up for that."

MacGuigan asked me if I felt that as legislators we should try to persuade our voters that the view we take on these public matters is the view that they'll have to take as part of their private morality.

"No," I said. "Just as I don't want to be hamstrung when I go into the House by the alleged view of my constituents, so too I would not impinge my conscience on the people who elected me. I am careful in observing the limitations of my role, which is a public role."

"Your question," MacGuigan said, "is how can just laws be formed on the increasingly complex life and death issues. To my mind, the politician deals with those issues only when he is forced to make a decision on them. He doesn't go out looking for them. I don't want to make decisions on the issues facing physicians today. I don't think that it's my duty to give ethical leadership on the life and death issues in advance of these questions being forced on me."

"That's a clear-cut position," I said. "But I disagree with you."

This exchange between MacGuigan and myself reveals the wide diversity of opinion among Members about what our role should be. It accounts for so much confusion about the "conscience" issue—whether M.P.s should vote according to their conscience or the dictates of a majority of constituents. In the cut-and-thrust of Parliament many feel that we should be happy if Parliament can keep the world from falling apart any more than it is. That is an accomplishment not to be diminished in an explosive world of confused values. But I want more from Parliament.

In my view the life and death questions affect the common good and belong in Parliament. The M.P. has a duty to propose his ideas and to vote according to his conscience in framing a law that is for the public good. Far from feeling inhibited from expressing his view to help clarify public understanding, he has a responsibility to give public leadership on the great questions that are affecting the dignity of human life in modern society.

The brilliant social analyst Hannah Arendt tells us that our traditional way of describing good and evil has become inadequate. Evil does not work in thunderous ways but is rather the silent accumulation of a thousand small decisions. It works geologically by erosion so that when the figure of devastation appears, the ground is ready. We can look at attitudes in this light. Because attitudes form slowly and, once formed, are hard to change or resist, it is essential that we attempt to influence one another early in the process. Thus today when we hear assertions that the good life is the "normal" life, about our right to discard people if they are inconvenient to us, we must speak. If we wait, the inevitable result of attitudes unchallenged in the formative phase will be dehumanization. What will the political process be able to do when these forces have run their course?

I spoke of Mickey at the beginning of this chapter and told how her life had deepened my understanding of what it is to be human. Who could say that Mickey's life has been wasted when she has taught her parents and perhaps others? I want to give Mickey the last word about normality in this chapter on life and death. And since she cannot articulate, I will let Jean Vanier, the friend of all the world's retarded, speak for her:

> Too long
> have we forgotten
> that Peter and John and Eileen
> —mentally deficient—
> are people.
>
> People who love
> and who want to be loved
> who have joys
> like you and me
> (you see we are normal
> . . . isn't it nice being normal?)
>
> —Jean Vanier
> *Eruption to Hope*

⟨ 7 ⟩

WHY I OPPOSED ABOLITION

In the middle of the 11 p.m. national television news on Monday, May 3, 1976, a picture of the hangman's noose flashed on the screen as the announcer reported the opening of the capital punishment debate in Parliament. "That debate wasn't supposed to start until Wednesday," I said to my wife Eva. I was at home in Edmonton, doubly annoyed because I had arranged my schedule to be present at the debate at the originally appointed time. My mood wasn't helped on the flight back to Ottawa the next day reading the newspapers that were deploring the fact that only fifty-three of the 264 Members were present for the opening of the debate.

I had gone to Edmonton for a round of appointments Friday in my constituency office and a weekend with my family. My capital punishment speech was going to be very difficult so I had stayed over to write it in the solitude of my study. But, as frequently happens, the government's legislative timetable went awry on Monday and Bill C-84, the measure to abolish capital punishment completely, was suddenly advanced. And so at 8 p.m. May 3 the Solicitor General of Canada, the Hon. Warren Allmand, rose at his second-row desk on the government benches to open the fourth full-scale debate on capital punishment in ten years.

In 1966 an inter-party resolution which called for the abolition of the death penalty and the substitution of a mandatory sentence of life imprisonment was rejected by 143 to 112 in a free vote. The government brought the issue back the following year with a compromise bill that would begin a five-year trial period of partial abolition; the death penalty would be removed except for the murder of a police officer or a prison guard. In another free vote the Commons approved this, 105 to 70.

By the time the first trial period expired I had come into Parliament in the 1972 election. In the spring of 1973 the government moved for a second five-year trial period and I voted for it. The bill passed, 119 to 106. The renewed trial period did not expire until December 31, 1977. Yet here we were in the spring of 1976, plunged into another torturous, divisive capital punishment debate.

Why? Because the government took a chance that the Thirtieth Parliament, elected in 1974, contained more abolitionists than retentionists. Thus Parliament would pass a total abolition bill and relieve the government of the nightmare of considering the commutation applications of eleven men convicted of murdering policemen or jail guards—in addition it would get the issue out of the way well before the anticipated 1978 general election.

During the trial periods the federal cabinet had commuted all five death sentences brought before it (in three of the cases the juries unanimously recommended clemency but there was no such recommendation in the other two). Although the cabinet has the statutory right to commute death sentences, the intent of the trial period was to provide only partial abolition. Parliament did not intend automatic commutation, which would be the same thing as total abolition. Rather it took the view that because of the extra risk in their work, policemen and jail guards should be given extra protection by sentencing their murderers to execution. The cabinet considered each of the five commutation cases separately but by arriving at the same conclusion each time, even when the jury had not recommended clemency, it gave the public the impression that it would not carry out executions, thereby effectively ignoring the present law. In fact the last executions in Canada were carried out December 20, 1962 when Ronald Turpin and Arthur Lucas were hanged back to back in Toronto's Don Jail. John Diefenbaker, who was then Prime Minister, signed the order permitting the executions to go forward even though he has been a life-long abolitionist. Public statements by

Allmand, however, that he would not be associated with an execution, further undermined public expectation that the sentences would be carried out.

The rising crime rate exacerbated the commutation debate. Violent crime in Canada increased 90 percent in the ten-year period 1965-74. In 1965 there were 243 murders in the country; in 1974 there were 545, the murder rate doubling from 1.2 per 100,000 population to 2.4. Despite the fact that 38 policemen and jail guards were murdered in this same ten-year period, no convicted murderer was executed. On top of all this the actual time served in prison by 42 murderers paroled between 1968 and 1974 averaged only 13.35 years. Is it any wonder that the public is losing confidence in the government's willingness to enforce the law?

All this was in my mind when I wrote to Warren Allmand in July, 1975. I had heard that the government was considering a total abolition bill as part of a package of new crime controls. The timing for a total abolition bill was wrong, I argued. Bring in a crime control bill, allow its effects to work their way through society by improving the statistics and reassuring the public on safety. Enforce the partial abolition law and repeat it for a third trial period. Only when the climate has improved and the public is ready to accept and respect a total abolition bill, should such a bill be introduced. "With so much fear in the air combined with lack of confidence in enforcement of sentences of criminals, it is no wonder there is such a strong public demand for the reinstatement of capital punishment," I wrote.

Allmand rejected my suggestion that total abolition be delayed, insisting that he was committed to changing the law in the present Parliament. "In your letter," he responded, "you state that you will vigorously oppose any change in the law at the present time. . . . That is your right and a question for your own conscience."

He was certainly correct in his "conscience" reference. Nothing has troubled me as much in my brief political career as the application of conscience on the burning moral issues of our time: capital punishment, abortion, nuclear sales, immigration, mass poverty, international development. The role of the M.P. in facing these moral issues is itself a principal moral question. I believe that establishing a correct priority of values to protect human life and dignity is the central question in our society today. Parliament is not the only place to conduct this debate but it is obviously the chief instrument in the conduct of the national public business. Unless Parliament can clearly create a consensus on these key moral questions, we are weakened in setting a course for the country.

A capital punishment debate reaches into the heart and emotions of the nation. It brings out deep feelings about the right to life, justice and the safety of society. The debate I entered in 1973 produced more mail, by far, than any other subject. I argued then in favour of the extended trial period of partial abolition because it would help to develop the climate for acceptance of total abolition. But the mail, running four to one against my position, indicated that my constituents wanted retention of capital punishment for all premeditated murder. Acknowledging that I was not voting the way my constituents wanted, I said in my 1973 speech:

> There is no way I can abdicate my responsibility to use my conscience in forming a decision as to how to vote. Some people think a Member of Parliament is a delegate to carry out automatically the wishes of the majority of his constituents, assuming the majority can be defined. But that is not my concept of the job. I believe a person is elected by constituents who repose a sense of confidence, for the time being at least, in his judgment and expect him to use it. The assurance that he will always vote according to his conscience is the best service that a Member of Parliament can offer his constituents.

When the Edmonton *Journal* carried a news story on my speech, the headline writer compressed my approach into these seven words: "Roche to buck voters on hanging issue." Another cascade of letters started, most of them blaming me for ignoring the desire of my constituents. "I would like an explanation of why you think you are better than your constituents who voted you into office to express their wishes," one voter wrote. Another said: "Please send me your reasons for voting exactly contrary to the wishes of the majority of your constituents. . . . These reasons will in effect tell me why you do not believe in the democratic system. Since you do not believe in democracy I think you should resign as an M.P. Your duty is to represent the wish of your voters, whatever it is."

Interspersed with the critical letters was the occasional letter of support for voting according to my own conscience: "We do not have a vote in the House of Commons; you do, and we elected you to vote according to your information and beliefs. We consider you to be our representative, not a conveyor of our votes. You could not be sure how your constituents would vote without taking a referendum and this is obviously impossible on each issue. Perhaps the supporters of capital punishment are the most vocal because they are the most angry, but we are not sure they are even in the majority."

To everyone who wrote me I replied that at almost every forum where I spoke prior to the election, I was asked my stand on capital punishment and gave it directly as being in favour of extending the five-year partial ban: "Therefore, my vote was certainly no different from what I had indicated before the election. I do not like to offend people, but I must do what I think is right. Unless I am allowed to do what I think is right in any given issue, I would never remain a Member of Parliament."

The hard test of this view, I realized, would be the next election. As a Conservative in Alberta I was not too worried about the outcome. But in 1974 my majority actually increased by 1,188 votes over 1972. The voters had not held my viewpoint against me.

But what would I do if the government pressed prematurely for total abolition before the end of the second trial period? When federal prison guards walked off their jobs July 2, 1975, protesting the steady stream of commutations of murderers of policemen or jail guards, I decided that the abolition issue had been raised to another level, which is respect for the law itself. It was this incident, plus the rumours of a new bill, that prompted my letter to Allmand.

People generally see the abolition of capital punishment issue in black and white terms. You're for or against. I was for abolition but I could not ram it down people's throats knowing their fears and frustrations about safety in society. I favour abolition because I believe in a morality that promotes the sanctity of life and excludes

violence and I feel that abolition is a step in this direction. But I am
not so rigid that I deny the state the right to take the life of a murderer. It is not inherently wrong for the state to impose capital punishment any more than it is inherently wrong to kill in self-defence or
in defence of one's country. By demonstrating that he is a threat to
society, a murderer may have to surrender his life if the common
good of society demands it.

The question is: *should* the state employ the death penalty? That
is what I have to make my judgment on as an elected politician trying to promote the common good. And while I wish for an abolitionist state, I have come to the conclusion that it is better, given all
the circumstances of society today, to keep capital punishment in
limited cases for the time being than to rush total abolition and
diminish public respect for the law. Is that compromising the principle of right to life or is it securing the protection of society? If that
is bending a principle, so be it. That is why I said above that abolition is not, for me, a black-and-white issue.

I decided to make my decision public early in the hope that my
vote might be one factor in the government's decision to delay the
presentation of a total abolition bill. The *Globe and Mail*'s Geoffrey
Stevens accurately reflected my reasoning: "Essentially, Mr. Roche's
argument was that the government has a responsibility to restore
public confidence in the administration of justice and the enforcement of criminal sentences before it tries to make abolition complete
—a step that would be bound to increase public concern." If the government could not retain the support of abolitionists like myself,
Stevens wrote, "it would be mad to try to change the law at this
time."

However—not for the first time—the government ignored my
advice. Immediately after the Progressive Conservative leadership
convention in the winter of 1976, Justice Minister Ron Basford and
Allmand teamed up to present a "Peace and Security Program" to
Parliament. The first measure, Bill C-83, provided for a more stringent gun-control program including increased penalties for people
who use firearms in criminal activity and the licensing of all pos-
sessors of guns and purchasers of ammunition. The sentencing pro-

visions of dangerous offenders, electronic surveillance and parole regulations were all tightened.

The second measure, Bill C-84, abolished the death penalty, replacing it with a twenty-five-year sentence for "first degree" murder. This was defined as planned and deliberate murder including "contract" killing, the murder of a policeman or jail guard, treason, and murder committed in the course of hijacking an aircraft, kidnapping and certain sexual offences including rape and attempted rape. "Second degree" murder, including murders of passion, would draw ten-year sentences. Although the twenty-five-year sentence for first degree murder was highlighted, a provision was included for a review of the parole eligibility date by three superior court justices after the offender had served fifteen years.

Although these two bills were separate pieces of legislation, they were sold to the public by the Basford-Allmand presentations as a peace and security package. What it boiled down to, the government declared, was this: the program was designed to provide better protection for the public against all violent crime, not just murder. And since capital punishment has not been proved to be a deterrent against murder, it should be abolished. A neat package—but it would not stay tied together. Immediately upon Basford's introduction of Bill C-83 on March 8, the Conservatives tried to split the gun control section (39 of 76 pages of the bill) away from the rest of the bill so that it could be voted on separately. Many Conservative Members supported the other crime control provisions but opposed the gun control section as excessively stringent. The government refused to split the bill. So many Members wanted to speak that the government saw its legislative timetable being destroyed; as a result the abolition debate would be so late that the cabinet would have to consider commuting the sentences of three murderers scheduled for execution July 15.

On April 13 after sixty Members had spoken on second reading, closure was invoked and Bill C-83 was sent to the Justice and Legal Affairs Committee. A whole new legislative battle was begun. Thirty-nine witnesses were called before the Committee and amendments by the dozen introduced. Although the final form of Bill C-83—

and certainly its long-range effects on society—was unclear, the government nonetheless rushed ahead with Bill C-84. It was committed to getting capital punishment out of the way regardless of the fate of Bill C-83.

Urging short speeches, Allmand gave a shortened version of his fifty-five-page written presentation in which he addressed himself principally to the almost sixty new Members elected since the previous capital punishment debate. "I am convinced," he said, "that if we attack this question objectively, then we must, from a logical, ethical and public policy point of view, conclude that capital punishment must be abolished once and for all." He advanced the argument that capital punishment is no more effective a means of protecting society than other less severe and less error-prone means. He referred to various studies, including a government-commissioned study by Ezzat A. Fattah, Simon Fraser University criminologist, showing that capital punishment is not an effective deterrent. Fattah wrote:

> Homicide rates . . . are conditioned by factors other than the death penalty. They suggest that the cause of homicide and murder cannot be found in any single factor but in a total social situation in which a special law or a particular punishment can have little or no effect.

From studies in Canada and abroad, Allmand told the House, "one cannot draw the conclusion that the prospect of capital punishment is a more effective deterrent to prospective murderers than the prospect of a life sentence. This is what it boils down to in the end."

Turning to the question of goals in society, he acknowledged that many people do not want capital punishment as an end in itself but as a justified and effective protection of society and the righteous expression of society's outrage against those who violate the right to life. But, he continued, it is precisely because it is an ineffective means that it should be discarded. In the past it has been applied disproportionately to those who are poor, unrepresented and members of minority groups. Capital punishment is irreversible and there is always the possibility of error. Moreover, juries are more reluctant to convict when the life of the defendant is at stake than when the penalty is one of fine or imprisonment. Thus the carrying out of executions by the state not only does not prevent murder but actually may serve to create or maintain a climate where more murders and more violence exist.

A twenty-five-year sentence, Allmand concluded, with a built-in rehabilitation incentive through parole eligibility after fifteen years is necessarily better than a sentence of death: "I am convinced that Hon. Members will see that the retention of capital punishment is not only ineffective but that it may actually be counter productive to the goal of protecting the Canadian public against murder."

As the Conservative critic of the Solicitor General portfolio, Erik Nielsen of the Yukon made his rebuttal by citing his own experience in World War II when fear of death was a relentless companion. Nielsen insisted that there is not one normal human being on the face of the earth who does not fear death. Death is a deterrent: "It may be over-simplistic, Mr. Speaker, but I believe that people will think twice about committing murder if they know that on conviction the death penalty awaits them." He also claimed that the same evidence put forward by the Solicitor General does not reveal that there is any more effective method of deterring murder than capital punishment: "You can go around in an ever-repetitive circle in the statistical argument."

Andrew Brewin then led off for the New Democratic Party giving an impassioned plea for abolition. He was followed by C. A. Gauthier for the Social Credit, a strong retentionist. The 10 o'clock adjournment came with Norman Cafik, the second Liberal speaker in mid-speech, building his case for abolition, and that was where the debate resumed Wednesday afternoon (Tuesday was devoted to an opposition day debate).

I had asked to speak early in the debate. On Wednesday morning, David MacDonald, a Conservative from Prince Edward Island and a strong abolitionist, asked why I was in a rush. I told him that even though I was holding to the principle of abolition I was going to oppose this bill. I had thought about the problem for nearly a year, had made up my mind and wanted to get my speech over with so that I would not be interpreted later on as caving in to public opinion when mail from constituents started. David disagreed with my stand and we argued vigorously for fifteen minutes in his office before going down to the House. He maintained that I had to be either for or against abolition. I held that the common good demanded respect for the intent of the law now on the books and that enforced partial abolition was still the best solution.

Immediately after the Question Period Eldon Woolliams, the Conservative justice critic from Calgary, protested that the scheduling of the Justice and Legal Affairs Committee's meetings on Bill C-83 would prevent Members from hearing the debate on Bill C-84. Parallel scheduling of committees with the hours that the House sits does keep attendance in the chamber down. But Woolliams' protest assumes that Members want to listen to speeches in the House— which is a long way from reality. As soon as the point of order was dismissed, the House cleared. There were four committee meetings scheduled, drawing a total of about eighty Members. When Cafik resumed his speech there were thirty Members present, four newsmen in the press gallery, twenty people in the public galleries— for this second day of debate in what was one of the most important and certainly the most controversial bills Parliament would debate in 1976.

David MacDonald followed Cafik and advanced a strong ethical argument: "The very desire to retain the death penalty is in itself a great affront to any individual who believes there is no higher value, in an absolute sense in terms of the duty of the state, than that of preserving human life." Not even the option of the state for capital punishment should be retained: "We cannot even for the sake of justice think of manipulating and abusing and occasionally executing people." I listened carefully because I have a great respect for David but I could not go this far in the rigidity of the abolition principle.

I was sitting in my back-row seat thinking about all this—a final time—while Réal Caouette, the Social Credit leader, gave his customary firebrand oratory in support of retention.

"I hear you're deserting us." I turned to the figure who had slid into the seat beside me. It was Gordon Fairweather, a long-standing abolitionist who was formerly Attorney General in New Brunswick. "That's not the way I would put it," I said, showing him my speech. He flipped through it, said nothing and left.

I realized immediately that my reasoning was not going to be accepted or even understood. Should I delay and think some more? No, I've thought enough. This is not the right time for an abolition bill. And didn't I have a significant quotation from Aristotle *(Politics: Book IV)* in my speech:

> The best is often unattainable, and therefore the true legislator and statesman ought to be acquainted not only with (1) that which is best in the abstract, but also with (2) that which is best relative to circumstances.

Caouette was finished. David Collenette, a young Toronto Liberal, was speaking for abolition. He had told me he would be brief. And at 5.20 p.m. the Speaker turned back to the Conservative side and I was on my feet. There was barely a quorum of twenty in the House. No need for oratory. Hardly anyone will hear, let alone listen to, the speech. Just get it on the record.

I explained why I thought Canada was not ready for total abolition.

> It might seem that, as one who hopes that Canada will one day be an abolitionist country, I would welcome this bill. But I do not. The government's action in bringing in a total abolition bill now is an underhanded way of evading its responsibility in carrying out the present law. It will be impossible to build public support for total abolition while the public thinks that the enforcement of present laws, including the partial abolition law, is too lax. We must move forward slowly, surely, and honestly if real progress is to be made . . .
>
> The public has a perfect right to demand the highest standards of safety in society; what the public sees is growing crime and weak law enforcement. It is in this climate that the government introduces a total abolition bill. What grotesque timing!

Since I am prepared to accept an inferior law at present, I posed, what should be the proper course for the government?

> It should apply the crime prevention bill as improved in committee, and then extend the present capital punishment law for a third five-year period. Let the public judge, on the evidence of its application, whether it is a good law. Only then should we be asked in Parliament to make a definitive judgment on whether this country should live under an abolition or a capital punishment law. But free us from political machinations in such a deeply moral question. The common good demands that we take more time in coming to a final answer.

The next speaker was Ursula Appolloni, a Liberal with whom I worked in the anti-abortion movement. "Mr. Speaker," she began, "I regret I should have to follow the speech of the Pontius Pilate on the other side of the House." Although I regard myself as reasonably hardened to criticism, the remark stunned me. Pilate had washed his hands of the blood of a man he acknowledged to be innocent. I was certainly not sentencing to death innocent men. Was my position so nuanced no one would understand it? Tired and discouraged I went back to my office. "Get the speech ready for a household mailing," I told my staff. "Let's hope people at home will at least read it before either damning or praising me."

The reaction started coming in quickly, especially with the Edmonton *Journal* carrying a front-page headline the following day: "Anti-abolition stand by Roche a surprise move." The *Journal*, in an editorial, dismissed my reasoning as "a tortuous explanation of an astounding about-face." My Edmonton secretary said the phone calls were in my favour, but as the mail started coming in it was clear that a lot of abolitionists were shocked and upset with me.

A constituent, Myron Johnson, wrote:

> What I find so despicable about your betrayal, what makes me ashamed to acknowledge that you are my M.P., is your utter hypocrisy and shameless opportunism in abandoning principle for short-term expediency.
> One would have thought that in your haste to abandon your unwarranted reputation for humanitarianism that you might

at least have been ashamed enough to attempt to come up with some reasonably plausible explanation. But your reasoning was so specious and your excuse so pathetic that one hardly knows whether to laugh or cry.

And this from John McInnis:

> I see that you have abandoned principle for political opportunity. I too have read the polls.
> There is no need for you to recant the twisted logic by which opposition to capital punishment can be translated into a vote against a bill to abolish capital punishment. Wrong is not right because a politician has found a way to attack the motives of those who propose right . . .
> Lest you think this note is too strident, too cynical ask yourself why this might be so. It is damned hard to escape cynicism and outrage when men of principle find a way to do the expedient thing.

The mail was not heavy, but the hostility expressed in letters like these indicated a belief that I was acting out of political expediency. Is it really impossible for an abolitionist to vote against Bill C-84 and maintain credibility? That became the central question in my mind. The Calgary *Herald* considered my speech so unusual that the paper printed the text of it. And in a follow-up article, Paul Jackson, parliamentary correspondent for both the Calgary and Edmonton newspapers, suggested that, despite my explanation, I was concerned about talk that unless I started paying more attention to the wishes of my constituents and less to the woes of the Third World I might be "either opposed for renomination or bumped off by a right-wing Liberal." So much for Aristotle.

Some of the mail cheered me up. "Thank you," wrote Mrs. L. E. Burford, "and if more Members were so honest and straightforward with their constituents we would have a more honest government."

The next day in the House there were four consecutive votes on a medicare bill immediately after Question Period. A total of 195 Members voted. The House moved right into the capital punishment debate and the exodus was so noisy that the Speaker had to interrupt

Leonard Jones, the independent Member from Moncton, to ask for quiet so that he could be heard. Three committees were meeting; the minutes indicate that a total of thirty-four Members were involved with these meetings. As soon as the House settled down and Jones resumed I noted there were twenty-three M.P.s in the House, one newsman in the press gallery and twenty people in the public galleries.

Flora MacDonald stopped at my desk to tell me how shocked she was at my speech. At that very moment, Walter Baker, the Conservative House leader, turned around in his front row seat to call up to me: "That was really a great speech you made." I started chuckling at the timing of these two comments. "Well, Flora," I said, "that's the way it is in politics. Some like you, some don't."

Jones took a hard line, expressing concern not for convicted criminals but for the victims of criminals: "Any threat of punishment—be it death, imprisonment, fine or chastisement at school—once recognized as a mere bluff obviously ceases to be a deterrent." He was followed by Jim Fleming, a Toronto Liberal and a member of the Canadian Society for the Abolition of the Death Penalty, who reminded the House in a well-planned rejoinder to the retentionists in the Conservative Party that our three consecutive leaders, John Diefenbaker, Robert Stanfield and Joe Clark, are all abolitionists: "Surely their judgment, which was considered as the basis for giving them the leadership of their party, is the same kind of judgment which has led them to be abolitionists." All day the speeches continued. Bill Jarvis, retention; John Gilbert, abolition; Robert Daudlin, abolition; Jim McGrath, abolition; Crawford Douglas, retention. What struck me was the thoughtful, moderate argument on all sides. Many Members, especially new ones, were clearly agonizing over their vote.

It was 4.20 p.m. the following Monday when I got back to the House from Edmonton. Stan Darling, the peppery Conservative Member from Parry Sound-Muskoka, was in full flight: "I say to the Minister of Justice and to the Solicitor General that their responsibility is not to the bleeding hearts, to the innovative, misguided social workers and the other assorted do-gooders in our society.

Their responsibility . . . is to millions of law-abiding Canadians who must wonder at times whether there is anyone on their side." A colourful speech. But again no audience. Thirty-three M.P.s, one reporter, five people in the galleries. I noted my Alberta colleague, Arnold Malone, striking a similar theme as mine: the government must first establish peace and security, satisfy the population and only then move for total abolition. Lincoln Alexander said he was impressed with that argument—but he would vote for abolition nonetheless. Simma Holt, the Vancouver journalist and Liberal back-bencher who is everyone's favourite (except possibly the Prime Minister's) for her outspoken independence, jumped in: "I enter this debate in opposition to Bill C-84. My position is that capital punishment must remain in the Criminal Code so that society, and society's agents, have the basis on which to move against killers who plan and carry out ruthless murder."

As the debate went on through the week the views of various churches were expressed from time to time. The Canadian Council of Churches had come out for abolition. So had the Canadian Catholic Conference. No church had denied the state the right to impose capital punishment, however. I had long ago decided that the Bible could be used, with isolated texts, to support either position. There can hardly be any doubt that Christ taught forgiveness and mercy, but he also taught justice. The difficulty of applying religion directly to the issue was illustrated when Alex Patterson, a B.C. Conservative and Minister of the Church of the Nazarene, and Andy Hogan, a Nova Scotia N.D.P. Member and a Catholic priest, spoke back-to-back. Patterson backed capital punishment; Hogan called for abolition. Patterson said that even though it is necessary to retain a system for severe penalties, society must do more to rehabilitate criminals. Hogan said that, although mercy and forgiveness are the essence of Christian teaching, he respected the right of people to favour the death penalty.

The most interesting of all the exchanges on capital punishment broke out on May 18 during the Question Period when John Diefenbaker asked Trudeau to retain capital punishment for treason. Treason is defined in the Criminal Code as killing the Queen, warring against Canada, or assisting an enemy at war with Canada, and it has always been punishable by death. When the British parliament abolished capital punishment for murder, the death penalty for treason was retained. Trudeau responded that the principle of abolition does not admit any exceptions. By removing the death penalty for treason in Bill C-84 the Canadian government went too far for abolitionist Diefenbaker. A few days later he reprimanded the government for this unwarranted "kindness to terrorists, international murderers and those who raise rebellion":

> Bring in the bill without that clause and I will vote for it. Bring it in in its present form and make Canada the Mecca . . . for all the thugs, terrorists, PLOs and Castros. As for me, my conscience will be clear when I vote against it.

By this time about seventy M.P.s had spoken and the argument on both sides was thoroughly exhausted. So were the Members who began to fear that the debate would force Parliament to continue sitting into July. The House leaders began dealing. Though at first the retentionists resisted extra hours in order to speed up the debate, the resistance weakened when the government put over the remainder of the Committee and House work on Bill C-83 until the fall. As far as I was concerned, that was one more reason to vote against Bill C-84; the vote on it—one way or the other—would be over long before the companion piece of legislation on crime control would ever be made law. The government stopped talking about the "package." A fundamental law of the political process was taking over: the closer the summer break looms the more reasons are found for doing things which were previously opposed.

Clearly Members were sick of the subject. When the Canadian Society for the Abolition of the Death Penalty held an evening seminar on Parliament Hill, only a handful of M.P.s came and they didn't need convincing since they were all abolitionists. The seminar was led by Arthur Maloney, the Ontario ombudsman, Bishop Emmett Carter, president of the Canadian Catholic Conference of Bishops, and Harold Veale, an Edmonton lawyer. When I took issue with them on the grounds that a climate for abolition should be built in order for the law to be respected, they responded that the public had been misinformed about the actual murder rate (the statistics failed to distinguish between premeditated murder and manslaughter). It was now evident to me that my stand, based on the timing of the bill, was neither understood nor accepted.

As the debate entered its final days the free vote aspect took on a critical importance for the government. On almost every piece of legislation the political parties take a stand and Members are expected to support their party. On the whole it is a good system because there is so much legislation that no individual Member can follow all the detail. A Member relies on caucus committees to recommend party positions and if he dissents he expresses his opinion in caucus. The function of the caucus discussion is to obtain a consensus and by voting in solidarity a party exercises as much power as it can muster. Sometimes an individual dissents from his party's vote. But not many votes provoke a decision based on one's conscience. Of the 226 recorded votes in my time so far in Parliament, not more than a dozen required that individual, lonely examination of conscience.

Bill C-84 was, of course, a free vote. Or was it? Since the bill was sponsored by the government, the twenty-eight Members of the cabinet decided to support it en bloc. What about ambitious government backbenchers reluctant to vote against the government? As the abolitionist headcounters did their work the word went out that the bill might lose unless those few Liberal M.P.s still wavering voted yes.

The full extent of the government's worry was revealed by the impassioned speech of Prime Minister Trudeau who rushed to the Commons immediately upon the adjournment of the First Ministers conference on June 15. Some M.P.s described it as one of Trudeau's finest speeches. He spoke very directly:

> I want to make it very clear that, if a majority of Hon. Members vote against abolition, some people are going to be hanged. Their death would be a direct consequence of the negative decision made by this House on this bill. . . . While Members are free to vote as they wish, those who vote against the bill, for

whatever reason, cannot escape their personal share of responsibility for the hangings which will take place if the bill is
defeated.

The more I reflected on this passage the more I objected to it. It
seemed to me that the Prime Minister was revealing here that the
government had no intention of carrying out executions under the
partial abolition law. He wanted a new law and if I didn't vote for
Bill C-84 and it was defeated, I would be partly responsible for
executions. I felt this to be intimidation. If the government did not
want to carry out executions under the partial abolition law, it
should never have introduced it. Surely the government had made a
mockery of the law, thus undermining public confidence in it. And
here was the Prime Minister now intimidating Members so that they
would back him in total abolition, the effect of which would be to
automatically commute the death sentences of eleven men convicted
of killing policemen and jail guards. That's not my idea of honest
government.

Even though I objected to what seemed to me to be desperation
tactics of the Prime Minister, I conceded that his speech generally
was perhaps the best defence of abolition in the long debate. He
argued persuasively that capital punishment has neither rehabilita-
tive, punitive, nor deterrent value: "It is because I have an enduring
confidence in mankind, and confidence in society's ability to protect
itself without taking human life, that I am eager to support this bill
and vote for the abolition of capital punishment." Eloquent as it
was, the speech ignored the whole argument about timing. I still
maintained that the climate for total abolition did not yet exist.

Two days later the debate ended. One hundred and nineteen
M.P.s had spoken for forty-six hours over nineteen sitting days. The
vote was scheduled for the following week. The newspapers were
predicting a cliff-hanger. A cross-over vote such as mine could be
determinative. When I was in my Ottawa apartment the next day
two of my close friends on Parliament Hill phoned to urge me to
vote for the bill. My reasons were not understood and were too
complicated, they said. I went back to the pile of Hansard speeches
on my desk. Again I came to the conclusion that the common good

demands that we take more time in coming to a final answer and that vigorous crime control legislation ought to precede abolition. I didn't claim to be absolutely correct in my judgment; I only knew that I was doing what I thought was right. The CBC phoned to ask if I would go on "Cross-Country Checkup" the following Sunday to explain my position "as an abolitionist voting against the bill because of your constituents' wishes." My nerves were a little raw and I blew up at the caller. "That's not the reason I'm doing this," I said, setting out once again the explanation.

The CBC program focused on the question of an M.P. following his conscience rather than on the merits of the issue itself. Most callers insisted that the M.P. should follow the wishes of his constituents which, of course, would result in retention. The final editorials and media coverage that I saw on the weekend were clearly biased in favour of abolition. The Toronto *Star* reported that the fate of the bill was in the hands of five undeclared Liberal backbenchers, Maurice Harquail, Antonio Yanakis, Tom Lefebvre, George Baker, and Claude Lajoie.

The vote was scheduled for June 22 at 12:30 p.m. When Parliament opened at 11 a.m. the public galleries filled up immediately and there were long lines outside. The press gallery was overflowing. All but three M.P.s were present: Albanie Morin was gravely ill, Erik Nielsen was stranded in the Yukon and Walter Dinsdale in Europe, a victim of the airline strike in Canada. Simma Holt, her left leg broken, came on crutches and Stanley Haidasz appeared with his head swathed in bandages.

There was no taunting back and forth as there usually is during votes as the clerks carefully counted the Members who stood to vote yes or no. True to his word, Diefenbaker voted no. Joe Clark, as he had said he would, voted yes. The five Liberal wavers split three-to-two, Harquail, Yanakis and Lefebvre voting for abolition, Baker and Lajoie for retention. In a few minutes the voting was over. For the bill, 133. Against, 125. The N.D.P. voted solidly for the bill, the Creditistes solidly against. Thirty-eight of the 139 Liberals voted no; eighteen of the ninety-five Conservatives voted yes.

When I got back to my office CFRN of Edmonton was on the

phone looking for my comment. "Are you breathing a sigh of relief?" the interviewer asked. "Why should I be?" I responded. I was starting to worry about the reaction of prison guards and policemen. I was fearful of strikes but did not want to say anything publicly. The Ontario police chiefs were furious and already demanding the government's resignation.

The members of the Standing Committee on Justice and Legal Affairs found notices waiting for them when they returned to their offices, summoning them to a meeting that afternoon to start study of the bill. The government was in such a hurry that the notices had been printed even before the vote was taken. The abolitionist strategy became clear: no witnesses, other than the Solicitor General, no request to the House to allow T.V. coverage, a quick handling of the bill to get it back into the House for report stage and third reading before public pressure could be mounted to change the votes of a few still-doubtful M.P.s who had voted abolitionist on second reading. The retentionists, led by Conservatives Eldon Woolliams, Allan Lawrence, John Reynolds and Sinclair Stevens, protested the "railroading" tactics which even went so far as to attempt to remove Simma Holt, a Liberal retentionist, from the Committee. Although the same committee had heard dozens of witnesses when considering Bill C-83 and its gun-control provisions (resulting in twenty-eight amendments), not even the director of the B.C. Penitentiary (where the turnover rate of guards is sixty per cent in the first year of employment) would be called this time. Yet a crucial aspect of the bill would be conditions inside prisons with the death penalty permanently ruled out. The steamrolling became ludicrous with the Liberal Members on the Committee, mostly Francophones, arguing that the Committee should sit on St. Jean Baptiste Day, a holiday in Quebec, and western Conservatives declaring they would not tolerate such a terrible disregard for French-Canadian culture. Not even the guarantee by the retentionists that they would limit themselves to a five-day debate on third reading if it were put over to the fall would dissuade the government from keeping Parliament in session as much of the summer as necessary to get the bill made law.

As for amendments (e.g. keeping the death penalty for treason or second-time murderers), the chairman, Mark MacGuigan, ruled out of order all but one on the grounds that they nullified the principle of the bill. The only amendment accepted provided for a jury, not a judge, to decide if a convict could be released on parole after fifteen years. This point touches on the most revealing part of Allmand's testimony. The publicity surrounding the bill highlighted the fact that the government was replacing the death penalty with a twenty-five year sentence for first-degree murder. The length of the sentence was intended to satisfy the public that murderers would be dealt with severely. But the bill contains a provision enabling a convict to apply after fifteen years for a reduction in the years he must serve before being eligible for parole. "For the fellow starting his sentence," Allmand said, "he does not know if he is going to get parole eligibility at fifteen or up to twenty-five." Under the present law, parole eligibility is fixed at ten to twenty years: *"The penalty for murder in this bill is not much different from the penalty for murder under the present law except for the fact that we are abolishing capital punishment* (italics mine)." So much for the government's campaign to convince the public that the penalties for criminal behaviour were being tightened up.

Six days (three of them being the St. Jean Baptiste holiday, Saturday and Sunday) after the second reading vote the bill was reported back to the House. The rules allow M.P.s to submit amendments irrespective of what the Committee has done and Mr. Speaker Jerome found forty-five amendments on his desk. He had no trouble ruling out many because they were in direct conflict with the principle of abolition. But other amendments were submitted under Rule 75(5) which permits the deletion of a clause within a bill. This is a very controversial rule since if a key clause is deleted it can have the effect of nullifying what the bill is trying to do. By a quirk in the rules, a Member is permitted to try to accomplish something indirectly that he could not do directly.

Altogether twenty-nine amendments were admitted into debate and at first it looked as if the whole summer would be required to dispose of them since theoretically every Member is entitled to speak once on every amendment. But the report stage debate quickly focused on the specific amendment introduced by John Reynolds. This amendment would have retained the death penalty for murdering policemen or jail guards—in effect maintained the status quo of the partial abolition period. If the retentionists could mount enough strength to have this amendment passed, Bill C-84 would be destroyed. But if the amendment failed, it would amount to a psychological defeat of the retentionists and take the steam out of the remainder of the debate. The showdown vote loomed for July 8 at 9:30 p.m. The amendment lost 132 to 117. The margin for total abolition had widened and the fight was over.

The remaining amendments were quickly disposed of; the only one accepted by Allmand requires the National Parole Board to give permission before a murderer is allowed escorted day leave from prison. A Liberal retentionist, Larry Condon, tried to delay the third reading vote by three months but the government would not allow even this concession. A final flame shot up from the dying embers when Claude Wagner accused Marc Lalonde in the House of shameful conduct in holding "a potent cocktail party" just before the critical report stage vote. As leader of the Quebec Liberal caucus, Lalonde had held a party but denied that he had attempted to influence Members in their votes. Wagner refused to withdraw his charge that "eight Liberal M.P.s, avowed retentionists, changed their vote under pressure." In a final speech Wagner also criticized Trudeau for attempting to "blackmail" the opponents of Bill C-84:

> I totally reject the allegations of the Right Hon. Prime Minister that, should Bill C-84 be defeated, those who voted against it will be responsible for the death of the murderers. None of us, including Members of the Cabinet, ought to feel guilty for action according to his conscience and enacting legislation to uphold social order and deterring the most hardened criminals from making attempts on the lives of others, especially policemen and jail guards. . . .
> The fact that the Prime Minister has thus attempted to personalize the debate, by pointing to eleven prisoners awaiting the gallows, proves how desperate is the situation in which he has placed himself by trying to impose his own wishes on Parliament and the Canadian people.

By now, however, no one was listening. Allan Lawrence made a vigorous speech accusing the government of having betrayed the country by rushing total abolition before the expiration of the trial period: "The majority of public opinion in the country is decidedly against not only what has been done but the way in which it has been done." I looked around the House; again there was barely a quorum.

When it came on July 14 the third reading vote was anti-climactic and practically a repetition of the second reading vote. The Bill carried 130 to 124. By six votes Warren Allmand had succeeded in making total abolition the law.

Back in my office I started going through the latest mail and found a letter from the Rev. L. E. Smith, a United Church minister in Regina who had been one of the ministers I consulted in Edmonton before entering politics. He found my position "ambiguous" because I acknowledged that capital punishment is inconclusive as a deterrent, yet I was willing to continue it as if it were an effective deterrent to rising crime. He felt that I had been "quite polemical" in charging the government with political manipulation. Nonetheless, he thought that I had voted correctly—"according to your present position on the matter; you are, when it comes right down to it, with the retentionist side."

Dr. Smith's letter convinced me that I had failed to communicate my position to him. There were other letters, however, that supported me. Barry Gates wrote: "Like yourself I am an abolitionist at heart but feel it is impossible to implement this kind of a policy at the moment in Canada."

The conflicting points of view in the mail drove me—once again—inward to the loneliness of facing a decision on a moral issue on which intelligent and honest men differ profoundly. Not even some of my closest friends could understand me. I should have made a better speech undoubtedly but I would not change my position. How could I vote for total abolition now when the social conditions for it are wrong? In politics, black and white positions are understood. But some issues are truly shrouded in grey.

❈ 8 ❈

THE LAWN BOWLERS DON'T LIKE ME

It is easy for a politician to get into trouble.

One day I received from the Department of National Health and Welfare, for my comment, an application under the New Horizons Program. This is a program through which the government funds projects originated by senior citizens. The application from the Garneau Lawn Bowling Club in my constituency sought $8,973 for the renovation of the greens, improvement of drainage and lighting facilities and another greens mower.

Not the weighty stuff of national issues, true. But I was annoyed. I wrote a letter to the Minister, Marc Lalonde, in which I suggested that the application was a perfect example of what is wrong in Canada today; increasing public dependence on federal funding for almost everything under the sun has largely been responsible for excessive government expenditure. In the four years I have been in Parliament federal spending has increased from $20.5 billion to $38.4 billion.

"What possible reason can be given for the federal government getting into the funding of a community operation like lawn bowling?" I wrote. "Somewhere we have to blow the whistle and stop this ridiculous expenditure of public money." It is not so much the New Horizons Program that I oppose as the philosophy that leads the government to spend money on recreational luxuries when the real need of so many senior citizens is more money for basic necessities. The precarious income position of the increasing section of the population over sixty-five is reflected in the fact that fifty-seven per cent of them have incomes so low as to require the guaranteed income supplement provided for old-age pensioners. Even though the Canada Pension Plan and the old age security program are indexed to provide more benefits as inflation goes up, senior citizens continue to find their savings and income eroded by inflation.

For some time I had been afraid of a backlash developing among people resentful of so much social spending on wide-ranging programs, including unemployment insurance and the Local Initiatives Program, a program administered by the Department of Manpower and Immigration to alleviate seasonal unemployment. I had become convinced that the increased social spending directed to people who may not need it deprives those who really deserve social benefits: "What we ought to be doing is increasing social spending for the disabled, disadvantaged senior citizens and all those in our communities across Canada who are not able to take care of themselves and to whom society has an obligation. Increase the spending for these special groups and decrease the social spending to people who do not need it." I concluded my letter to Lalonde by supporting efforts toward "a more humane society in which those who are able to work are given sufficient economic opportunities and incentives and those who are unable to work are given money."

I released the letter to the press. And then the roof fell in. Lawn-bowling senior citizens attacked me for my insensitivity to their recreational needs. They asked why I wasn't fighting big grants to commercial sports enterprises instead of picking on them. Several senior citizens were hurt that I had singled them out in my money-saving campaign. "What could be more enjoyable to the older folk on a sunny afternoon than lawn bowling followed by a social time over a cup of tea in their most modest clubhouse?" wrote one person.

The Edmonton *Journal* seemed bemused at my "latest excursion into the realm of the unique" in resisting a grant for my own constituency: "That makes him a non-conformist of the first order, since by custom an M.P. is a representative of the people who does battle for his own while reserving the right to demand that belt-tightening be practised anywhere but in the old home town." But *Journal* readers were not amused and the letters were against me. M. Patricia

Coughlan wrote: "His time and efforts would be better served if Mr. Roche sees to it that our senior citizens get a full share of the wealth their past efforts helped to provide. His vehemence against such a reasonable request is, to say the least, dismaying."

The lawn bowlers did not need to worry since a few days later the government announced approval of the grant. I went to the next meeting of the Standing Committee on Health, Welfare and Social Affairs to speak directly to the principle I was trying to highlight. With a slight smile Marc Lalonde noted, "I am not surprised at the reaction that Mr. Roche received from the senior citizens in his own area and I will leave him to handle this particular question." To the applause of the Liberals on the Committee he said that the Edmonton grant was a good investment in the morale of senior citizens that would "save money in health care, depression and isolation."

I talked over the case the next evening with my friend and parliamentary colleague Dr. Bob Holmes. "I'm using this case as a symbol of the wrong kind of federal spending," I said. "Forget it," Bob advised. "Your constituents don't understand that kind of symbolism."

There is a great debate going on in Canada about social spending. Inflation has brought the issue to everyone's attention. It is no longer a matter of choosing free enterprise or socialism, controls or no controls, initiative or welfare. The welfare state has already arrived and the common good demands that it be reconciled with the protection of human initiative. We need to examine how much control our economic and social system requires in order to protect the quality of life and consequently how much federal government intervention Canadians want. I see around me people paying ever-higher taxes to support an ever-growing government apparatus and yet the problems of transportation, housing and safety in society are getting worse. Distrust of a large, powerful and faceless bureaucracy in Ottawa is intensifying.

It is the absence of clearly defined social goals in government planning that has led us to the present cumbersome bureaucracy in which government spending at all levels occupies 38.5 per cent of the gross national product. We continue to add programs (and a civil service army) to take care of exigencies without any clear idea of what kind of society we want.

Government spending at all levels will exceed fifty per cent of the economy within a decade. Provincial expenditures are rising fastest of all, principally because the provinces are administering more social security benefits which are direct off-shoots of the federal government's economic and social policies. The trend in our society is toward an economy dominated by government. The increasing intervention of the state in our economic and social life is leading to further dependency of the people on government and is diminishing initiative in the further development of Canada. Personal tax rates will continue to rise in the next few years to pay for the present system.

The combination of slow growth, trade deficits, high inflation and unemployment rates and zooming public debt have angered Canadians and made us fearful of the future. We are trapped. As long as the economic pie keeps growing we can all hope for a bigger share. But when the pie doesn't grow we continue to fight for bigger slices. In this climate any talk of a new society, new values or sharing exacerbates the resentment. Yet the debate is essential. For we are fooling ourselves if we think we can spend our way into some sort of just future. We must recognize that more federal spending is not the answer to either unemployment or inflation. And it has certainly not brought justice to those least able to fend for themselves, the focal point of my concern in this chapter.

My $8,973 lawn-bowling issue is tiny indeed, a pebble on a huge beach of federal spending. The Department of National Health and Welfare, which spends twenty-eight per cent of the federal budget, has an appropriation of $10.9 billion. Most of this money is used up in transfer payments, which are taxes collected and redistributed in the form of grants, subsidies and support of individuals, organizations and other governments. Examples of transfer payments are old-age pensions, family allowances and hospital insurance and medicare programs. Both rich and poor benefit from these universal programs. Only five per cent of the Department's budget goes to direct cash payments to the poor, although these payments are bitterly attacked in some quarters as being excessive.

If absolute poverty (in terms of basic survival needs) is decreasing, relative poverty is not. The Canadian Council on Social Development reports that between 1961 and 1973 "the real income position of the poor has not increased relative to that of the average Canadian." Statistics Canada reports that in 1965 the bottom 20 per cent of the income scale for all family units received 4.4 per cent of the total income and the top 20 per cent received 41.4 per cent. Six years later in 1971 the share of the bottom 20 per cent fell to 3.6 per cent, while the share of the top 20 per cent rose to 43.3 per cent. While incomes advance for those who can run the race, they lag behind at the bottom levels of the working poor. The poor are not receiving a higher proportion of the wealth than they were two decades ago. Today 3.5 million Canadians still live in poverty.

Thus the hitherto sacred principle of universality is now being called into question and a more selective approach to social spending examined. Does it make administrative sense to give free services or cash to 100 per cent of the population and then reclaim it—or more correctly, part of it—by taxing back from the seventy per cent who are not poor? By providing equal benefits for all, a system promoting equality is not only terribly wasteful and inefficient, but actually encourages the retention of inequalities. As Senator David Croll, who headed the Senate's investigation into poverty, says, "There is a call to conscience in this land of ours. . . . No matter how we redistribute income—whether by taxation, fiscal arrangements, capital gains, transfer payments or tariffs—in a very short time the same people end up with all the marbles." The economy grows and everyone is supposed to be better off. This "trickle down" theory, in which the poor are supposed to be automatically better off when the rich get richer, does not work. What this most recent period of rapid economic growth has meant for the low-income wage earner is simply that prices rise faster than his wages (the control program notwithstanding) and, relative to meeting his needs, he becomes poorer.

The solution therefore is to devise methods of ensuring that people who need help are identified without involving demeaning individual investigations or crippling administrative costs for the state. What is required is an income-return form which automatically indicates whether the individual qualifies for aid.

My experiences in Parliament have shown me some of the real problems which are caused by the inequalities of our present social spending program. One of my best lessons occurred the day I talked to George Goodman (not his real name), one of my constituents.

A tall man with a plain face and a strong voice, Goodman had called me to complain that he was going to lose his Canada Pension Plan medical benefit because he had obtained a part-time job with a project under the Local Initiatives Program. "Why are they doing this to me?" he shouted in anger and bewilderment. "Are they trying to put me on welfare?"

Gradually I put together the basic picture of his life. For many years he had been a pig farmer about fifty miles south of Edmonton. But the arthritis that had troubled him periodically for several years eventually became crippling and he had to sell the small farm and move to the city where he could get hospital treatment. Canada Pension awarded him a disability pension of $140 a month, his wife took a job and, at age sixty, George Goodman faced a bleak future.

Only by real frugality were he and his wife able to meet their monthly bills but with inflation it was apparent that they soon would not be able to keep up. Goodman had the choice of applying for welfare or finding a part-time job that he could manage. His health was deteriorating and he had to spend increasing amounts of time in a wheelchair. But it was easy to see that Goodman was a proud man and that welfare would be the last measure. He heard of a LIP grant to a handicapped group in Edmonton that was setting up a workshop to produce artifacts. The group gave Goodman a part-time wood-working job at $45 a week. He reported his intention of taking the job to Canada Pension which immediately warned him that he would jeopardize his pension. Goodman was furious and so was I. In fact, being relatively new on the job as an M.P., I couldn't believe that any government agency would be so stupid as to penalize a pensioner for increasing his income by working when the alternative was welfare.

I went downtown and talked to the local manager of Canada Pension, a pleasant fellow who confirmed Goodman's story and then doubled my amazement by admitting that he could do nothing about the case; the decision would be made by "a committee in Ottawa." To my argument that this kind of impersonal, centralized bureaucracy was exactly the kind of thing that was alienating people from the federal government, the official shrugged his shoulders. While agreeing with my criticism, he was powerless to change the system.

After leaving the manager's office I wrote a strong letter to an official in Ottawa, protesting the basic injustice of taking away Goodman's pension. In the end Goodman got to keep his pension and started work on the LIP project. But after a few months Goodman was back where he started. The project's funding ran out because LIP was set up to create temporary jobs during winter months when unemployment is high. Goodman's condition was not related to seasonal factors. He needed a subsidized work program the year round.

The more I probed into LIP the more I saw that it had become, all across the country, a vehicle for social groups to plug into because they could not get funding for work programs anywhere else. I saw handicapped groups creating work projects out of LIP funding only to have their hopes for self-help dashed after a few months when the program expired. I saw senior citizens panic-stricken because they had become dependent on food and other service programs that were financed under LIP and now were about to be cut off. I resent the fact that the socially and physically disadvantaged in our society are so desperate for the means to financial livelihood that they are forced to grasp at whatever straw is offered. In the case of Goodman society has an obligation either to pay him a disability pension on which he can live decently or create an employment opportunity with permanent funding and administered at the community level, not the federal.

The defenceless people of our society—the handicapped, aged and working poor—need someone to speak for them. Not just a lonely M.P. They need our social system to speak and act for them. To say that is to say a mouthful since it is our economic principle of relentless growth which develops and perpetuates poverty and insecurity. Our way of life is geared only to those who can keep up with the demands made by our economic system. Our philosophy, well intentioned as it is, is to legislate for the health of the system and then hope that somebody takes care of the casualties.

Taking care of the casualties has now become a "big business" itself. Our society has become a very complicated, expensive welfare state without any signs that the root causes of poverty are being stamped out. There is such a jumble of policies, programs and jargon that only specialists (and probably not too many of these) can keep from being overwhelmed. No wonder politicians are inclined to take the easy way out: approve another program to take care of another need. Thus to keep peace in a troubled economy vast amounts of the social budget are directed to people who do not need it while the truly unemployable are miserably short-changed. Because we continue to think that economic casualties can be treated with social bandaids we tolerate a system that is not only humanly unjust but a financial nightmare.

Who are these economic casualties? They are the chronically unemployed, the unskilled, the poorly educated, the minority groups of Indians, Metis and Inuit, the disadvantaged, infirm, aged, one-parent families, inhabitants of depressed areas. For these people poverty has become a way of life, "an ugly sub-culture within Canadian society," as the *Senate Report on Poverty* put it. Generally they have inferior educational, medical, cultural and information services and lack the skill or knowledge to make use of many of the facilities available to the general public.

The greatest tragedy is the children of these people who grow up in a cycle of poverty. "To be born poor," the National Council of Welfare says, "is to face a greater likelihood of ill health—in infancy, in childhood and throughout your adult life. To be born poor is to face a lesser likelihood that you will finish high school; lesser still that you will attend university. To be born poor is to face a greater likelihood that you will be judged a delinquent in adolescence and if so, a greater likelihood that you will be sent to a 'correctional institution.' To be born poor is to have the deck stacked against you at birth, to find life an up-hill struggle ever after." The poor are certainly not understood by the rest of us nor do they get much of our sympathy. We think they should be able to meet the prevailing social norm, which is competitive survival of the fittest. It does not occur to many of us that we ought to change our prevailing social norm to one of cooperative interdependence which would provide more extensive opportunities for human development.

Unequal opportunities and their divisive consequences are evident everywhere. Canadians on fixed incomes must bear the burden of ever higher living costs but corporate profits keep climbing. Adequate housing is beyond the reach of this "subculture" but land speculators and developers continue to reap profits. A quarter of the population must struggle for the basics of food, clothing and shelter but those who provide these get rich. Many families find it impossible to erase their debts but finance companies and banks prosper.

These disorders stem from a distortion of values. The value of the human being is measured by his ability to buy (and hence consume). Those who are materially poor have failed. Measuring the worth of persons by their income level and buying power encourages social discrimination that compounds the harm. A subtle discrimination segregates rich and poor in housing developments, schools, law enforcement and health care.

It is easy to enunciate a clear principle of justice: every member of Canadian society has a right to a share of the national wealth sufficient to enable him to participate fully in society. But it is very difficult to put this principle into practice while there is so much public confusion and resentment of the present social security system.

It is not the government but the initiative of free men and women that enables most people to work out their own destinies. People should be encouraged to be dependent on themselves rather than on the government. This, rather than the perpetuation of government handouts, is the route to a life of human dignity for the poor. Therefore Canada's goal must be the creation of greater income-earning potential among the poor themselves. When this principle is accepted there should be public support for permanent community employment programs, better training programs for the unskilled and retraining for workers in declining industries.

What is especially offensive is that there are so many people who find that taking a job at or near minimum wage will provide them with less disposable cash income than they can get from the social security program. For example, a 1973 study in Ontario showed that the maximum welfare payment for a family of four was $375 a month. A person working at the federal minimum wage of $2.25 an hour earned $378 a month, which was then subject to standard deductions, tax, Canada Pension Plan, unemployment insurance. The worker also had to pay transportation and clothing costs. But the welfare cheque was not subject to any deductions and the recipient very often also received free dental care, free eyeglasses, free prescription drugs and medicare. It was estimated that in Metropolitan Toronto for every person on welfare, there were two persons who worked and took home less than they could get on welfare.

This is certainly unfair to the working poor. Senator Croll estimates that there are half a million Canadian workers in this position: "The Canadian people have a right to require the acceptance of the work ethic. But have not those who comply with the work ethic the right to ask for a decent job with a living wage?" The wonder is that anyone in poverty does work. That so many do is a strong indication that the work ethic is not dead. But unless courageous action is taken, the spiralling costs necessary to prop up an ineffective welfare system will perpetuate dissatisfaction and bitterness among both those who give and those who receive.

Sometimes I am asked if my criticism of the inhumane competition of the capitalist system does not reveal that I am a socialist at heart. I do not think so because the increasing state ownership of socialism implies a rigidity which stifles human initiative and independence. Inevitably the power of the state becomes excessive under socialism. I also cannot believe that the complete welfare state a socialist administration would produce would lessen the financial burden. Indeed the present discontent in Sweden revolves around the taxpayers' revolt against the heavy costs of the welfare state.

I look for a system of economic humanism in which there are sufficient controls to protect the common good while leaving people free to seek their own destinies. It is not government handouts, whether in cash or programs, that will ameliorate the plight of those with low incomes. It is difficult for a politician to argue against higher family allowances, higher pensions, more unemployment benefits and more welfare benefits, which are the principal responses of the federal government to income disparity aggravated by raging inflation. Yet this approach augments the cost of government, bringing the bill for social bandaids to a dangerously high level without closing the gap between rich and poor. Rather than perpetuating the welfare system we ought to concentrate on employment programs which would raise job incomes thereby making more money available for the truly disadvantaged.

The working poor (who comprise at least two-thirds of the poverty population) are very often trapped in low-paying jobs because they are not equipped to rise in our competitive economy. It would be more fair if we recognized the necessity of low-paying jobs to the production process and the lack of control an individual has over his productive contribution. Thus the 1973 federal *Working Paper on Social Security* proposes a wage supplementation program, based on family size, for the working poor. A long process of federal-provincial consultation has been searching for methods that would protect national norms while leaving the provinces free to legislate benefits at not less than a minimum level. The National Council of Welfare regards wage supplementation as a possible major breakthrough in reducing poverty in Canada.

The core of the wage supplementation idea is that there always be a financial advantage to working. Accordingly a worker's income, if below the established poverty line for a family of his size, would be boosted by the government (either through direct payment or a negative income tax).

Another idea also advanced by Senator Croll and others is to help the working poor who are not organized with a government-sponsored package of benefits that would help to dignify work: a minimum wage, a guarantee of that wage as long as the worker is willing to work and does work, medical and dental insurance, disability insurance, prescription drugs. In other words the worker would have all the benefits and most of the protection that his unionized brother has. Recognizing that there are few incentives for employers to provide these work benefits to the less qualified, Senator Croll urges the government to provide the common fringe benefits and security: "What the working poor need is a substitute for the market power of the trade unions, for the political and economic muscle which they possess. Big business can look after itself, and big labour can look after itself, but the rest cannot and they need help. This help can only be supplied by the government—not to bargain with employers, but to bear the cost of the commonly acceptable fringe benefits—in return for production that saves it on welfare and unemployment insurance payments." This certainly is an approach to strengthening the work ethic and redistributing income and wealth more equitably.

Community employment programs, wage supplementation and government-sponsored benefits for the working poor are creative solutions to poverty. They are vastly superior to the present chaos in which the blurred line between welfare and the working poor produces frustration and bitterness.

What I have described above seems to me to achieve the same end as the much-discussed and much-feared "guaranteed annual income." The very phrase should be abandoned by all social reformers because it conjures up false notions of able-bodied people receiving money whether they work or not. The proper concept is one of social justice—no one seeking to participate in society will be allowed to receive less than a minimum income to enable him to live in human dignity. The working poor must be given more incentive to work and the state of the public treasury demands that we plug the welfare sieve by supplementing working incomes rather than giving out "free" welfare payments. In this same positive framework we can encourage business and industry to take those steps necessary to make work more inviting in a computerized society: shorter work weeks, reorganized production so that workers can vary their labour and learn new skills and worker participation in management.

The test of Canadian integrity is met finally in our treatment of the unemployable people in our society—the aged, the handicapped and retarded. Why we should have to argue that these people deserve our justice, not our charity, is itself a commentary on our underdeveloped social consciences. We provide pensions and supplementation allowances but we seem to be afraid to tackle this problem head on and declare that society has an obligation to support, at least at the minimum poverty level, all those who through no fault of their own cannot earn their living.

I would call this a guaranteed annual income for the unemployable. It is inexcusable not to guarantee these people an income by right rather than make so many of them apply for social assistance which puts them in the welfare category. In Edmonton a group of handicapped people put on a drive for funds and went canvassing door-to-door. I find it disturbing that handicapped people are not sufficiently protected so that they would not have to consider such measures. They met a cool reception from the public, clearly upset at this visual confrontation of society's neglect. The situation of the aged poor is not very different. I see the aged regularly throughout my constituency trying to scrimp by on old-age pensions that, despite indexing for inflation, are inadequate.

I want more money for the unemployable so that they can live in the dignity to which they are entitled—not as cast-offs from our economic machinery. It is nearly impossible to solidify this necessary, permanent boost in their income as long as a big percentage of social security money is siphoned off to support programs for people who need only an opportunity to develop their own lives.

Social analysts appear to agree that a cornerstone of a new social policy would be the establishment of community employment programs. The government took an initial step in 1975 with a three-year experimental program of twenty pilot projects for those who experience chronic unemployment: the handicapped, retarded, ex-inmates of mental or correctional institutions and single parents who cannot work outside the home. Since this program is capable of creating permanent employment, it could fill a social need at the local level and give an expanded definition to the traditional concept of work. Government-created work is growing in acceptance despite the mishandling of the Local Initiatives Program and the Opportunities for Youth Program that have been the leading examples of new-style community work. Provided they are permanent and de-centralized from Ottawa, community employment programs deserve support because they are a progressive step toward ensuring employment opportunity for all Canadians.

If society wishes to call any activity work and pay for it, it should be able to do so. Perhaps if mothers and homemakers were rewarded directly, there would be less desire to seek a "legitimate" job outside the home. Along with Dr. David P. Ross, income security director for the Canadian Council on Social Development, I feel it odd that "our values in society lead a mother to feel that putting labels on deodorant bottles in a factory is more virtuous and useful than tending a child at home and administering to his unique intellectual and emotional needs. It certainly appears to answer the question as to whether people or goods are more highly prized by our society." Thus a new concept of work should embody the belief that a community's output of goods and services should have more personal services than are now provided through the private market mechanism.

A simplified, more equitable social security system is essential. The principle is clear: maximize benefits for the unemployable; maximize opportunities for the employable. The planning required for these goals necessitates guidelines for society. We need social indicators to help us understand the inter-relation between economic and social development. This is especially necessary when social spending is held back in a period of economic restraint. The principle social indicators that are regarded internationally as a measurement of the quality of life are: health, individual development through learning, employment and quality of working life, leisure, command over goods and services, physical environment, personal safety and the administration of justice and social opportunity and equality.

If we had a Social Council of Canada using these indicators to measure our national progress, it would enlarge our perception of social wellbeing. Social indicators would complement a field which has been left almost exclusively to economics and to material indicators of progress. Social indicators would also help to remind us that economic progress may have serious non-economic consequences. The price of profit may be too high.

The real problem is who makes the final decision on weighing indicators. Parliament should be involved in the development of values which would give direction to social indicators. It is certainly the role of Parliament to promote social harmony and justice in a world being fractured by disparities. Politicians should be actively engaged in the examination and articulation of social values. We must be particularly sensitive to the qualitative as well as the quantitative aspects of Canadian life.

The Canadian Council on Social Development provides four objectives for social revision: significantly reducing income inequalities; equalizing opportunities and increasing access to those opportunities that allow individuals, families and groups to enhance the quality of their lives; expanding work options; and increasing the participation of people in the making of decisions that control their lives. For its part the National Council of Welfare reduces social justice to two objectives: guaranteed employment opportunities and guaranteed income adequacy for all Canadians. A foundation for these goals is a social policy at least equal in importance to economic policy.

Dr. Ross points out that the great debate over the work ethic reveals two basic questions. First, should the individual adjust to the economic system, or should the economic system adjust to the individual? Second, why should only that activity performed in the economic marketplace and paid a direct wage be regarded as legitimate work? Is not homemaking and parenting a work activity? To ask these questions is to challenge the growth and private profit objectives of the present economic system and throw the spotlight on the development of a system where concern for the individual is foremost.

A more human society cannot be brought about by unfettered individualism. The changes which have occurred in our lifestyle as a result of the relentless march of technology have produced common problems for society. They can only be solved by an orderly co-operative approach in which the individual and special interest give way to public concern for the common good. As Harleigh B. Trecker points out in *Goals for Social Welfare, 1973-1993*, "The individual must be seen and understood in society in a much more complete way than in the past. The intervening act of helping must focus not only on the individual but on the *interaction* of the individual in his groups and in society. Many of the pressures on the individual are societal in origin and no amount of working on or with the individual alone can relieve these pressures. Society must be changed."

This means concentrating on problem-producing factors such as unbridled technology, planless urbanization, unresponsive government and the selfishness of those who control the economic system. In my mind all of this is connected not only with raising the quality of life domestically but helping Canada to play a stronger role in an international community devoted to obtaining universal peace, freedom and justice.

⟨ 9 ⟩

WHAT THE WORLD NEEDS NOW

Eleven a.m. May 31, 1976. Queen Elizabeth Theatre, Vancouver. For an instant everything came together. The analysis of global problems which cause mass poverty, the solutions and the motivation to act. Habitat, the United Nations Conference on Human Settlements—but actually about the whole of life—was about to begin.

One of a series of U.N. world conferences during the 1970s on the environment, population, food and women's rights, Habitat was billed the most important and largest U.N. meeting ever held. It would be a jamboree of speeches, ideas, politics, films, parades and exhibits. A parallel conference for the public called Habitat Forum would encourage public participation. There would be so much going on that Habitat would require its own daily newspaper (the media centre registered 1,490 journalists).

Now at the Queen Elizabeth Theatre the government delegates from 134 countries took their places at the long rows of desks. The interpreters in sound-proof booths were waiting to translate every word into the conference languages—English, French, Spanish, Russian, Arabic. Canada's Governor General Jules Léger was escorted to the stage. At the Canada desk, Barney Danson, Secretary of State for Urban Affairs, waited to be formally called to the platform to assume the presidency of the conference. Across the stage strode the Secretary General of the U.N., the tall and dignified Austrian Kurt Waldheim, who was ready with his challenge: to help 500 million people living in misery, ill-fed, ill-housed and struggling every day to survive. "The very magnitude of the problems facing us," he declared, "and the fact that they are beyond resolution by anything less than a concerted global effort, must act as our dominant impera- tive. . . . We are talking about people—where and how they live, about the quality of their lives, and about the future for themselves and for generations yet unborn."

The star of the opening ceremony was undoubtedly Canada's Prime Minister, Pierre Trudeau, who came to talk about love. Using the cosmic theologian Teilhard de Chardin as his guide, Trudeau appealed for a "passionate love" of our global neighbour based on an unprecedented desire to change ourselves. His speech aimed high: " 'Love one another or you will perish,' writes Teilhard in *L'énergie humaine*, adding that we have reached a critical point in human evolution in which the only path open to us is to move toward a common passion, a 'conspiracy' of love."

An hour later the same theme of love was struck by Mother Teresa, the saintly nun from Calcutta, who addressed an overflow crowd at Habitat Forum held at a converted seaplane base called Jericho Beach four miles from downtown Vancouver. Appealing for an outpouring of love to bring bread to the hungry, to clothe the naked and provide homes for the homeless, Mother Teresa said in her simple manner, "Let us not just put this love into words, let us love until it hurts."

A little while later I was discussing with a Canadian external affairs officer these sublime themes which had been meant to lift delegates at both Habitat conferences above the short-run politics of the problem. "Love is all very well," the official said with a smile on his face, "but protect your ass, that's what you have to do at these conferences."

Down to earth.

This cynical comment, born of attending too many international conferences, turned out to be a more accurate description of Habitat, as it lumbered through two weeks of torturous politics, than the opening appeal for love. In fact Habitat ended in the bowels of Mid- east hatred when the Arab states forced a climactic vote by brand- ing Zionism a form of racism. The Declaration of Principles, toward

which Habitat was aiming, could not be passed by consensus because of the Arab intransigence in using Habitat to bring attention
to the political problem of the Palestinian refugees. Habitat was
consequently branded a failure by many journalists. I would not
describe Habitat as a success. But to find the real reason for its lack
of success we must examine more of the changing world scene than
just the Mideast enmity. As we do, a new role for Canada and new
commitments in our foreign policy will become apparent.

First of all, what was Habitat trying to tell the world?

One-third of the entire urban population of the developing world
lives in slums and squatter settlements. Forty per cent of the people
in the developing world do not have water within a hundred metres
of their homes. More than half the people in developing countries
have no electricity. Those are just the opening statements in the
description of a world scene in which hundreds of millions of people
in the thirty-five least-developed countries, now called the "Fourth
World," live in conditions of absolute poverty and deprivation. They
form a global ghetto which is becoming increasingly isolated from
the rest of the world. And in many Third World developing countries where dramatic economic growth has occurred, the benefits of
this growth have not reached the poorest of their people.

The problem of urban growth has now become explosive. In the
past quarter century nearly 300 million people in the developing
world have abandoned their rural birthplaces and migrated to the
urban centres. Governments have been unable to stem this tide because the migrants believe that the terrible conditions to which they
move are still better than the conditions they leave behind. This is a
desperate choice. I still remember the day that Aristides Bastidas, the
Venezuelan journalist I described in Chapter one, took me through
the wretched slums and filthy squatter settlements on the hills surrounding Caracas. I saw there, as I have seen in other developing
countries, the human degradation that gives a flesh-and-blood meaning to the incomprehensible statistics.

In 1950 there were seventy-five cities of one million population,
fifty-one in the developed world and twenty-four in the developing.
Today of 191 "million" cities, 101 are in the developing world. The

super-cities now are predominantly in the developing world where, according to the U.N. figures, ten of the seventeen gigantic agglomerations of "ten-million" cities will be located by 1985. In short, the twelve fastest growing cities in the world are in the developing countries. With these cities hopelessly unable to meet the demand for physical and social services, human catastrophe lies ahead. In all these areas a small minority enjoys an exotic level of comfort and consumption while the masses of the people are unable to fulfil their most basic needs.

Meanwhile the countryside is not being deserted. Despite the tremendous transfer of people to the cities, the rural population is rising and will continue to do so because of the overall population growth. With half the world's population today under the age of twenty the additional people who will demand housing, services, jobs and food in the next two decades are already among us. This crisis is not only a question of housing or inadequate transport systems or urban pollution and congestion. It is, says Enrique Penalosa of Colombia, who was Secretary General of Habitat, "a crisis of social organization and of civilization itself." That is why the U.N. conferences have pointed to the necessity of a global strategy for development at this critical moment in history.

Though difficult for most of us, it is essential to look beyond the horizon in order to understand what is happening to modern man. One of the central facts of the world today is that the economic growth of the twenty-one most heavily industrialized countries is leaving far behind the one billion people in the thirty-five poorest countries. The problem of extreme poverty is perpetuated by the control which the developed world exercises over the bulk of the earth's wealth. The one-third of humanity in the developed nations consumes more than sixty per cent of the earth's resources. A baby born in Canada will grow up consuming fifty times the resources and energy that a baby in the developing regions will consume. This implies that the developed world is responsible for a much greater per capita environmental impact than the less developed nations. In taking for granted ever higher standards of living, the minority of rich countries get richer at the expense of the multiplying poor. That is not a formula for peace or security in a world already on edge over resource depletion and spreading nuclear technology.

Anyone who advocates narrowing the gap between the rich and poor nations, while at the same time envisioning a continued three to five per cent increase per year in real income for the bulk of the people in the industrialized nations, is supporting two irreconcilable policies. Sustained growth in the western world can only be maintained by paying low prices for commodities, protecting domestic industries and increasing production of consumer goods, which would in turn demand more resources. Merely to maintain their economic growth the industrial countries must continue to appropriate a totally disproportionate share of the world's raw material and energy output. Redistribution would only be possible if the developed nations were willing to accept a new style of life. There is not much chance of this happening as long as the industrial economy of the West is built on expansion and greed.

Our approach to global justice should not start from the negative position of merely deploring the massive poverty and suffering in the developing world today as if there were nothing we could do beyond applying bandaids. Rather we should recognize the new, positive values of interdependency. Biological and physical interdependencies, inherent in the basic structure of our planet, are now accompanied by a network of manmade interdependencies which are changing the fabric and mechanics of our life.

The acceleration of scientific and technological developments has opened up the possibility of maximizing the physical, mental and social wellbeing of everyone. Instruments probing the solar system have helped to develop a planetary science which enables us to better understand the physical structure, life chemistry and stabilizing systems of our planet. The detection and study of solar energy, climatic changes and atmospheric pollution will eventually contribute immeasurably to man's survival no matter where he lives. There are now more than a dozen countries with their own satellites; telecommunications and education are within the reach of hundreds of millions previously isolated. Joint space programs have already led to legal treaties.

World-wide data collections on the biosphere's conditions have been launched by governments under the U.N. environment program. Rapid technological development of the seabed has led the U.N. to declare the sea (beyond the limits of national jurisdiction) a common human heritage. Atomic energy, electronics, computers and cybernetics, plant genetics and engineering, industrial agronomy, antibiotics, microbiology and laser technology—all these developments have profound implications for the non-industrialized part of the world.

Once we grasp the concept of interdependency, we see the actuality of it in more and more places. The movement of trade, agricultural production and use of energy all require new commitments and mechanisms to better explore, distribute and manage the earth's resources for the benefit of the whole population, present and future. The relationship between economic activity in the highly industrialized centres and in the developing countries is at the core of world economic stability. The impact of world public opinion and international organizations is already felt in the call for a code of conduct for transnational corporations which themselves have scaled national walls with ease. Though transnational corporations are often and correctly characterized as exploiters, they have shown that a transfer of skills and technology, properly utilized, can introduce new areas of the world to industry.

The value of interdependency becomes more apparent as we see that religion, race, culture and social mores no longer have to be insuperable barriers keeping people apart. The extensive interplay today of diverse ideas and personalities through travel and communication is bound to affect our behaviour. I am not claiming that a utopia has arrived, nor am I closing my eyes to the tragic conflicts which continue to scar the earth. But I see, as a result of interdependency, the evolution of a stronger civilization as we motivate mankind's knowledge, imagination and organization toward the creation of a civilization of stewardship and restraint.

Many people despair at what appears to be the hopeless task of sharing the world's resources and recommend "lifeboat ethics" by which the rich decide to save some and leave the rest to drown.

While I believe that compassion still outweighs cynicism in public opinion, the terrible complexity of achieving distributive justice is producing a scepticism which in turn feeds our selfishness. If we can't do anything about poverty, why care?

The problem of global survival is not a lack of resources but a distortion of values. A moral will to apply evenly the benefits of technology, rather than simply expanding technology, is our greatest need today. Do we have the courage necessary to preserve our sensitivity, awareness and responsibility in the face of radical change? For as Rollo May writes in *The Courage to Create*, "We are living at a time when one age is dying and the new age is not yet born". It takes creative courage to discover new forms, new symbols and new patterns in which a more humane society can be built. The old age was one of narrow, nationalistic self-interest. The new age is one of global interdependencies. We do not yet know how to cope with the demands of a new planetary civilization, so naturally we resist it. But the movement toward some kind of world order is inescapable. What is now imperative is the structuring of a new global ethic, one dedicated to providing enough food, shelter, education and health care for every human being on earth along with the opportunity to live in self-fulfilment.

In May, 1969, U Thant, then toward the end of his ten years as Secretary General of the United Nations, made this prophetic statement:

> I can only conclude from the information that is available to me as Secretary General that the members of the U.N. have perhaps ten years left in which to subordinate their ancient quarrels and launch a global partnership to curb the arms race, to improve the human environment, to defuse the population explosion, and to supply the required momentum to world development efforts. If such a global partnership is not forged within the next decade, then I very much fear that the problems I have mentioned will have reached such staggering proportions that they will be beyond our capacity to control.

As we consider the issues isolated by U Thant—the arms race, environment, population and world development—we quickly see why the hope I expressed above must be balanced with some hard realities.

There has been absolutely no progress made toward ending the arms race. Despite *détente* the arms race has moved onward and upward since 1969 and today the world spends almost $300 billion annually on arms. Six nations belong to the nuclear club and the number will soon reach ten. The two super-powers have sufficient overkill to annihilate each other's populations ten or twenty times over. There is no prospect of disarmament.

There has been some progress in protecting the human environment, chiefly because of the growing political awareness of the need to conserve resources, including energy. Although the new U.N. environment agency is a step forward, the economic depression has resulted in the postponement of tougher regulations in some places.

Concerning population, it is now clear that the problem of the developing countries is not over-population as such. The 1974 World Population Conference in Bucharest emphasized that large populations are not the cause of underdevelopment but the result of underdevelopment. In the developing countries couples still want many children because they fear that several may die and they need children to work and help support them as they grow old; children become the substitute for material and financial security. Thus family planning programs are only effective when they are part of an overall plan to promote rapid economic and social progress. Because poverty is the main cause of the massive increase in population, it is poverty that must be eradicated. There will then follow a sharp decline in the rate of population growth. But since the rich-poor gap is actually widening, the present world population of four billion will likely double by the year 2000 and probably not level off until the year 2030 when there will be between eleven and fifteen billion people.

This brings us to the fourth issue which must be dealt with if a future for mankind is to be ensured—world development. In 1960 the average income (gross national product per person) in the developed nations was ten times as large as the average income in developing ones but by 1972 it was fourteen times as large. The World Food Council estimates that 460 million people are either starving or malnourished. There are 200 million people unemployed. Some 75,000 people a day are migrating to already dangerously over-crowded cities.

The worst cases of cyclical deprivation are found in the Fourth World, the thirty-five countries most severely affected by the inter-national economic upheaval of the mid-seventies. Short of food, energy and fertilizer and trying to cope with the highest population growth rates in the world, they can only be regarded as economic hardship cases. They include India, Bangladesh, Pakistan, Burma, Ethiopia, Zaire, Tanzania. Their per capita GNP is $149 compared to $3,720 in the industrialized countries of the First World.

Examining for a moment just one of these countries, Tanzania, reveals why the Fourth World is increasingly dependent on foreign aid. In addition to coping with two years of drought Tanzania's petroleum bill has quintupled since 1973 from $20 million to $100 million, about one-ninth of the national budget. The increased prices of manufactured imports, caused by the rise in the cost of energy and other raw materials, have followed a similar path. But Tan-zania's principle exports—coffee, sisal hemp, cotton, tobacco and cashew nuts—have not risen in value. In fact the sisal market has nearly collapsed in the last year. The country's balance of payments has developed into a major crisis: increased foreign aid is used up in debt repayment rather than being used for development.

All this in a country many regard as one of the best development prospects in Africa because of the moderate and coherent policies of President Julius Nyerere who leads a government reasonably free of corruption and elitist showpieces. If Tanzania cannot become a developed country, we must ask what development does require. When we start to dig beneath the surface we see the connection be-tween poverty and systems that perpetuate poverty.

Grim as the catalogue of misery has been at international confer-ences, it has achieved a significant gain in the dawning recognition that the major crises of our time are not unrelated. The problems of food, population, employment, industrialization, urbanization, resources and environment are now recognized as symptoms of the same sickness—economic and social maldistribution.

Mihajlo Mesarovic and Eduard Pestel in *Mankind at the Turning Point* emphasize that "the whole multitude of crises appears to constitute one single global crisis of world development . . ." International cooperation is now a prerequisite for peace and stability so that the world can continue to evolve. Investigating in depth this global malaise, the Dag Hammarskjöld Foundation concluded that the food, energy and capitalization problems "are only the most obvious signs of a great disorder under heaven." The situation cannot be properly understood, much less transformed, unless it is seen as a whole: "In the final analysis, the crises are the result of a system of exploitation which profits a power structure based largely in the industrialized world, although not without annexes in the Third World."

The U Thant theme returns to haunt us: either cooperation or world chaos. What is clear, the Hammarskjöld Report insists, is that the existing order is coming apart "and rightly so since it has failed to meet the needs of the vast majority of peoples and reserved its benefits for a privileged minority. The task is to create another one. This will not be possible without a clear identification of the often divergent interests at stake, without struggle and without eventual transformation."

The primary purpose of economic growth should be to ensure the improvement of conditions for all. Every individual should have access to the necessities of food, shelter, education, employment and health care in order that he be allowed to develop his true potential and dignity in keeping with the common good. A growth process that benefits only the wealthiest minority and maintains or increases the disparities between and within countries is not development. It is exploitation.

For the past fifteen years the United Nations has been trying to build the political will to institute more equitable economic and social systems. There have been hundreds of conferences but it took the monetary collapse, the oil crisis and the famines of the early

1970s to awaken politicians who unfortunately often respond only to confrontation on their doorsteps. Rich countries discovered that the discussions and negotiations are no longer about how much aid will be given but about the structural changes that must be made in the monetary and trading systems of the world. These changes are all spelled out in the New International Economic Order passed at the Sixth Special Session of the U.N. General Assembly in May, 1974 and reaffirmed at the Seventh Special Session in September, 1975. The new economic order begins by stating its aims—"to correct inequalities and redress existing injustices and ensure steadily accelerating economic development, peace and justice for present and future generations"—and goes on to outline specific programs for international trade, industrialization, science and technology, transfer of resources and food production.

The developing countries want new sharing arrangements of the world's wealth and resources. The rich nations view these reforms with considerable suspicion—a natural reaction since the present systems are regulated for their advantage. Countries which depend on the importation of cheap resources from the developing nations will not look favourably on new regulations that will result in their paying more for the resources. On the other hand developing nations are not likely to sit still much longer while the added value of their exports of primary commodities is absorbed by western middlemen. So hard confrontation and tough negotiations are inevitable before any substantial movement toward the new economic order is achieved.

The new economic order calls for a linking of the price of raw materials exported by developing nations to the price paid by them for imported manufactured goods; the rich countries reply that prices must be allowed to reflect "market" forces. The new economic order demands some overall agreement and international regulation of commodities; the rich countries call for a "case by case" approach and the retention of controls by national governments. The new economic order calls for the use of the International Monetary Fund as a development instrument; the rich countries defend its use as a central bank regulating currencies and international liquidity. The new economic order calls for the regulation of transnational corporations in the interest of developing countries; the rich countries defend the rights of these corporations.

Against this vast background of social disparity and political manipulation I find myself, one politician, trying to cope with an overload of information and no buttons to push. All I can do is argue that this issue ought to be centre stage in Canadian foreign policy and try not to be too despondent or frustrated when I see how little attention is paid to it in Parliament. When I think of how much time and resources are spent in government and Parliament on the running battles of power politics, it convinces me that our political ideology lags far behind the reality of the changing world. The Economic Council of Canada was right when it pointed out: "In our increasingly complex, interdependent society, short range ad hoc responses to the problems of growth and change seem increasingly inappropriate in most instances."

It seems evident to me that Canada ought not only to have an integrated, comprehensive policy to respond to interlocking global problems but that such a policy ought to be given a high priority. For Canada can play a much greater international role at this turning point in history. In fact the global situation is thrusting upon us new opportunities as well as responsibilities; with a unified approach we can help developing nations become self-reliant and acquire stronger trading partners as a result. "Enlightened internationalism," as Professor John W. Holmes put it in *Canada: A Middle-Aged Power*, is going to cost more but it is the only realistic policy with which to respond to the new major issues—distribution of resources and population in the world at large. "What we have to note," he says, "is that the thrust is towards a principle of international sharing and it is directed against those countries which have the most resources and space per capita. The heat may be turned off the super powers and on the rich, middle-power, middle-aged countries like Canada."

In fact the heat *is* on Canada. The developing world regards us as a "fat cat." We like to look good at international conferences but without straining our economic relations with the major western powers—particularly the United States—that do not accept the new order. Canada's posture is ambivalent. We recognize our role as a bridge between the various factions but we do not exert leadership because we are neither convinced of the validity of structural changes nor have we determined what form they should take. Moreover, there is very little public support for such changes. Hence we stumble along with bits and pieces of programs with the various departments of government operating from totally different perspectives.

Most Canadians still think of our help to developing nations in terms of "foreign aid." The Canadian International Development Agency, administering about $1 billion annually in government funds (.52 per cent of our gross national product), has a high profile. CIDA's food, construction and service programs have undoubtedly helped countless people in the developing world. This work is still needed. But we should not delude ourselves by thinking that aid is an important economic factor in the developing world. It is not. The size of the problem dwarfs aid as an element in the transfer of resources. Neither should we think that Canada's aid is all that altruistic. Our direct, bilateral aid to the ten main receiving countries* in 1974-75, with a total population of 937.4 million, was $330 million. Of this, sixty per cent ($198 million) was spent on Canadian goods and services through tied aid (a regulation requiring a receiving country to spend the bulk of "aid" on Canadian goods and services). Canada's trade balance with the same ten countries in 1975 was a surplus of $368 million. Even allowing for the intricacies of trade figures, it is clear that monetarily, Canada is a greater beneficiary of our economic relations with these countries than are the developing countries themselves. Moreover, aid is not a high priority in government. When the government took an axe to its spending programs for the 1976-77 fiscal year, one would have thought that the poor of the world would be spared the cruel irony of a restraint program—especially since the Canadian defence budget was not cut. But the government slashed CIDA's spending plans by imposing a

*India, Bangladesh, Tanzania, Pakistan, Indonesia, Niger, Ghana, Tunisia, Sri Lanka, Nigeria.

ten per cent growth limit whereas twenty per cent growth had been the norm over the past few years. Hardly anyone noticed.

On the other hand the government has taken a modest step forward in the publication of its Five-Year (1975-80) Canadian Strategy for International Development Cooperation. Although weak in specifics, the Strategy is the beginning of a "multidimensional" policy, meaning that Canada intends to move forward on commodity agreements which will benefit developing countries, trade liberalization and industrial cooperation. Increased aid (but without a target date) is to be directed to the poorest countries, with the middle-income Third World countries being the first beneficiaries of the structural reforms. All of this falls well short of the new economic order but is at least movement toward it.

The Five-year Strategy begins by acknowledging that Canada, as one of the most prosperous nations in the world, has both the responsibility and ability to make a meaningful contribution to the improvement of conditions in the developing world:

> As a country with an impressive resource base, Canada has generally benefitted from the sharp rise in the prices of primary commodities. Shortfalls in world food production, in particular, have increased our grain exports and the prices paid for these on the world market. It is thus inevitable, no matter how badly we may view the domestic situation, that in the eyes of a hungry developing world Canada will be singled out in the future by the rest of the world to assume a great responsibility to share its food and agricultural commodities with the developing countries, as only one of four net food exporting nations.

Besides—and here the Strategy reverts to the self-interest argument —the development assistance program "can have catalytic and positive effects on the Canadian economy." Because there is so much emphasis on tied aid, the goods and services procured in Canada strengthen industry here, create jobs for Canadians, maintain support for the aid program and develop interests in overseas markets. As the Strategy admits, these benefits mean that the cost of the aid program to Canadian society is less than volume alone would suggest.

Because all this requires a great deal of study, I pushed in Parliament for the creation of a Subcommittee of the Standing Committee on External Affairs and National Defence to examine Canada's new role in international development. In an interim report issued in the spring of 1976 just before the Fourth United Nations Conference on Trade and Development (UNCTAD), we urged the government to exert leadership "in seeking creative solutions to the problems of commodities trade which will be acceptable to producers and consumers in both developed and developing countries." Because nearly eighty per cent of their foreign exchange income results from the export of primary products, the international market price of such products is of critical importance to developing countries. But these prices vary widely and unpredictably, and in times of world economic recession they sink below the price of the manufactures, food and oil products that poorer countries must import. In 1975 the purchasing power of primary-product exports from developing countries declined thirteen per cent.

UNCTAD has stressed this central problem and proposed a package agreement whereby the price of ten basic commodities (coffee, tea, rubber, copper, tin, cocoa, sugar, cotton, jute and hard fibres) would be stabilized by means of the international purchase and holding of reserves or "buffer" stocks of these goods. Our subcommittee suggested that an appropriate Canadian initiative would be a phased, coordinated approach toward increasing and stabilizing the prices of commodities by establishing a schedule for negotiations and new mechanisms to link commodity agreements such as integrated or common buffer-stock financing.

What the Canadian government did at the opening of UNCTAD IV was merely to repeat our familiar position that we were "prepared to continue examination of the proposal for a common fund. . . ." Yet the Scandinavian countries and the Netherlands were able to go into UNCTAD and immediately pledge a commitment to the common fund principle around which the success of UNCTAD was clearly seen to turn. The United States stuck by its proposal for an International Resources Bank which would increase private investment to help stabilize commodities. The U.S. proposal reveals the fundamental disagreement on development between the U.S. and the developing nations. The common fund would be a new trading structure; the bank proposal would only be an extension of present structures. The developing nations emphatically want new structures, not just the adaptation of old ones.

Only when pressure mounted did Canada go along with a proposal to set up a negotiating conference on a common fund. The mood at UNCTAD was bad because the developing nations (known as the Group of 77, although they actually comprise 113 countries) interpreted the western hesitation as a rejection of the nuts and bolts of a new economic order. In turn they voted against the U.S. bank proposal, a move that hardened the U.S. position against the new order. Instead of the cooperation hailed by the rhetoric of the Seventh Special Session, the relationship of the developed and developing world has fallen back to confrontation.

Modern events are forcing the developed countries to face up to new, hard questions. Does progress for us constitute ever-increasing production and consumption, while progress for the developing nations means providing only the minimum requirements of life? This was the kind of question raised in a unique tour of Canada I made with two other Members of Parliament, Andrew Brewin of the N.D.P. and Irénée Pelletier of the Liberals. As three M.P.s of different parties, acting on our own, we travelled across Canada from Halifax to Vancouver for ten days in January, 1976. We spoke to more than 2,000 people and met with citizens' organizations, religious groups, non-governmental organizations and representatives of government, education, agriculture and business. Our insistence that Canadian involvement in international development ought to transcend partisanship was a unique feature of our road show. Jack Webster, the Vancouver hot-line "Voice of British Columbia," couldn't get over our unified approach. "Imagine," he kept telling his listeners, "three M.P.s sitting here agreeing with each other instead of fighting."

The question of "putting our own house in order first" was a dominant reaction everywhere we went. Translated this means that we Canadians should take care of our own economic problems before we try to help the world. But experience convinces me that this approach—growth for us first, justice in the distribution of benefits later—is wrong.

Although there is some concern in Canada about social and economic disparities in the world, most people still think that more effective distribution and use of aid are all that is required. The proprosals of the new economic order and, indeed, Canada's own Five-Year Strategy, are practically unknown. It was this very aid-centred approach that Brewin, Pelletier and I tried to enlarge by emphasizing that Canadians have to cooperate in revising structural changes of trade and pricing systems rather than contenting ourselves with sending a few slices of bread to a starving child. The cost of this wider effort will depend on our willingness to pay higher prices for the primary products of developing countries and our willingness to allow more imports into Canada of manufactured goods from developing nations.

There is little public opinion in Canada to support this effort. "We're underdeveloped right here in the Atlantic area," a Nova Scotia educator told us. "We might get hurt if international buffer stocks of food are created," a Saskatchewan farmer said. "My friends work in the oil industry," a Calgary woman said, "and I can't get anyone interested in the Third World. They all think food is ripped off in the black markets and they don't want to support CIDA."

It was clear to us that Canadians generally are not in a sharing mood. Self-concern is the dominant viewpoint. While we found little overt opposition to foreign aid, confusion about its effectiveness prevails. Canadians may not yet be cynical about the suffering of the world but scepticism has overtaken compassion as a national characteristic. Many Canadians still believe that the breeding habits of the poor are the problem, not realizing that over-population is caused by poverty and cannot be controlled without rapid and sustained economic and social development.

As a sign of hope for improved Canadian motivation, we noted individuals and organizations speaking and acting against the national trend of scepticism and self-concern. They are a creative minority reflecting a profound view that the people of the industrialized world must adopt new attitudes toward consumption and stewardship of resources and the environment.

The Social Justice Committee of Montreal gave us a brief supporting higher commodity prices as a means to close the gap between the rich and poor nations. Seven Calgary students pressed us to take a moral stand on foreign aid, to stop devising aid programs of primary help to the Canadian economy and to meet "the true needs of the less developed world." The Nanaimo International Development Education Association urged vigorous promotion of the new economic order in Canada by first "exercising restraint in our personal lifestyles rather than to find ourselves enmeshed in spiralling demands far beyond individual material needs." Ann Holden, a thirty-four-year-old wife of a forester in Blueberry Creek, B.C. who has worked for ten years under CIDA contract in West Africa and Sri Lanka, called for less rhetoric in the Canadian approach and more sensitivity by CIDA to long-range development.

The representatives of non-governmental organizations (UNICEF, CUSO, Canadian Crossroads International and so on) were certainly the best-informed on development issues. This led the M.P.s to conclude that non-governmental public education programs ought to be stepped up considerably to fill the appalling gap in public information. This requires more money—one reason why the portion of CIDA's budget devoted to national and international non-governmental organizations ought to be increased.

We ended the tour convinced that the media in Canada, in fulfilling their social responsibility, should be providing much more information to Canadians concerning the new possibilities for international development offered by the new economic order. Why, we asked ourselves, does every Canadian know about the anti-Zionist resolution at the U.N. but hardly anyone knows about U.N. development plans? We also want the federal government to take its own Five-Year Strategy seriously by publicizing it (which is one of the points of the strategy itself). How can the public will be mobilized for a better effort in development without a firm basis of understanding? What is the purpose of having a Five-Year Strategy if no one knows about it?

The development story isn't all gloom and doom. Joe Winkelaar gave us all a great lesson in communication when he stepped to the microphone in Kelowna to sing his little ditty:

Snowmobile fell apart—outboard motor won't start,
Second car needs a new set of rings,
Summer house should have paint—Lord I'm goin' to faint
'Cuz I'm sufferin' from too many things.

Humour, unfortunately, is hard to find in this subject. That is why I relished the Winkelaar brand. But there was certainly nothing humorous in the approach of Luis Echeverria who, as President of Mexico, came to Habitat to upbraid the industrialized nations for their persistent "deep mistrust" of the proposals for a new economic order. And that brings us back to Habitat itself, as a focal point for the modern political drama of human development. As Echeverria told the delegates, "This conference is part of the great theme of our times, the division of the world into a bloc of abundance and an enormous archipelago of poverty." His was a speech of anger, a warning that the developing world is running out of patience, that serious confrontation lies ahead. The fact that it was given on the same day that Trudeau delivered his oration on love drove home the width of the gap between rhetoric and action. These excerpts reveal the growing mood in the developing world:

> The attitude which the industrial states have recently adopted in economic matters reveals the extent to which their real dispute is waged not in the sphere of world-wide ideological conflict but rather in that of specific economic interests . . . When matters come to a head, questions of profit and loss have always proved more powerful than the standards of freedom, democracy, justice and solidarity . . .
>
> In spite of the gravity of these problems the fourth UNCTAD in Nairobi showed that possibilities for any concerted world action between the powerful countries and the Third World nations to jointly implant a new international economic order are becoming dangerously remote . . .
>
> The accumulation of poverty is leading to a dead end from which escape is possible only by means of qualitative change. If we do not make these changes through negotiation and understanding, we shall inevitably be led to violence . . .

Habitat did produce a program of action for settlement planning. Dozens of ideas and programs for the construction of dwellings, ownership and use of land, water systems, rural development and community enterprises were built into the final documents. Through the sharing of information—as well as inspiration—many delegates gained confidence that the infrastructure of parks, schools, libraries, sewers and roads can be managed. Methods of arranging security of land tenure, establishing a transportation network and delivering water supplies were all shown on the screen. Habitat came out strongly in favour of public participation in community planning and for major clearance and renewal projects only when renewal of existing neighbourhoods is not feasible. The conference urged that "quality of life" criteria be major determinants in community design. These ideas have been promoted by planners (often regarded as radical) for years. But it was at Habitat that the ideas were given government sanction on an international basis. National governments were urged to crack down on land speculation and protect agricultural land.

It is a mistake to think that there is no public opinion in the developed world calling for real change, although on the whole the thinking reflected at Habitat Forum, the parallel conference for the public, was far in advance of public opinion in Canada. The Vancouver symposium, which was held in conjunction with Habitat (led by twenty-four internationally known development experts including Barbara Ward, Maurice Strong, Buckminster Fuller and Margaret Mead), issued a declaration demanding firm government control over land use, the securing for the community of unearned increment from land sales, the reinforcement of intermediate cities and rural settlements to create systems which strengthen agriculture and lessen the pressure on the biggest cities, a priority for the provision of clean water and introduction of conserving and recycling services, a moratorium on the adoption of nuclear technology and emphasis on solar power.

A group of representatives from Canadian non-governmental organizations backed up the Vancouver symposium's demands by urging the Canadian government to lead in establishing new international agreements regarding trade, monetary systems, industrial strategies and resource development programs which are advantageous to the developing countries. The non-governmental organizations want land treated as a community resource and not as a market commodity (a principle that should be reflected in control of land speculation). They also called for a moratorium on the expansion of nuclear power and a dollar commitment to clean water programs.

All this enabled Habitat to offer hope to the dispossessed of the world. The resolutions, if turned into actual plans, may give millions of people a more human life. But these accomplishments were lost in the politics of Habitat and it is the politics of development that are by far the major continuing problem.

The most important instrument to come out of Habitat was intended to be the Declaration of Principles which might develop world public opinion. A Declaration of Principles, a U.N. practice, loses its effectiveness if it has to be voted on. Therefore every effort is usually made to arrive at a consensus so that the world can be told that the U.N. has "unanimously agreed" that certain steps be taken.

As we have seen, Habitat was about much more than building settlements. Consequently the Declaration of Principles was an all-embracing document containing many hard statements that the industrialized nations are by no means ready to accept. Here is but one of the controversial points in Habitat's declaration: "To achieve universal progress in the quality of life, a fair and balanced structure of the economic relations between states has to be promoted. It is therefore essential to implement urgently the New International Economic Order . . ." It is precisely because the major industrial nations, including Canada, are resisting "a fair and balanced structure" of economic relations that it would be a mockery to give empty assent to that principle. The whole development debate is turning on the need for controlled international structures to override the inequities of market forces. The United States, for one, regards control of the market forces as unacceptable and perhaps unconstitutional and sees the continued pressure of the Group of 77 as an attack on the American system.

Canada, despite having accepted nominally the theory of a new order, balks at the practice and is too closely tied economically to the U.S. to do any pioneering. Canadian officials are deeply concerned that any "radical" changes will have adverse effects on our domestic economy (e.g. dislocating industrial and employment patterns) with consequent electoral backlash. Jean Marchand, former Minister of the Environment, admitted this openly in a press interview at Habitat. The government, he said, would risk defeat if it implemented the changes called for by the Group of 77. The voters are hardly calling for these changes to be made.

When the Arabs insisted on incorporating into the Declaration of Principles a section obliquely derogating Israel,* the United States found an easy way to avoid voting against the substantive principles it could not support. It merely suggested the document be voted on as a whole; under the pressure of the clock, that proved a popular suggestion. Consequently Canada (and fourteen other nations) was able to declare opposition on grounds of the racism section alone. The headlines that racism killed Habitat were, in effect, a smoke-screen covering the deep cleavage between the developed and developing countries. Predictably, public opinion in the industrialized nations reacted against the U.N. system for allowing itself to be dominated by Third World delegates so consumed with racial hatred that they would wreck the very conference that was designed to help them. The sentiments expressed by Gerald Leavens of Downsview, Ontario, in a letter published in the Toronto *Star* were echoed throughout the country:

Not only did Habitat not justify the money and energy spent on this sham of a world conference on housing, but one also begins to doubt the intelligence of pouring millions of our

*The key paragraph read: "Human dignity and the exercise of free choice consistent with overall public welfare are basic rights that must be assured in every society. It is therefore the duty of all people and governments to join the struggle against any form of colonialism, foreign aggression and occupation, domination, apartheid and all forms of racism and racial discrimination, *referred to in resolutions adopted by the General Assembly of the United Nations.*" The final clause (italicized) was considered to amount to a pointed reiteration of the 1975 explosive General Assembly resolution linking Zionism with "racism."

hard-earned tax dollars into the hands of the leaders of most of these Third World countries.

Instead of countries like India helping their poor and desperate millions to help themselves, they prostitute themselves and their votes in international organizations for the sake of Arab approval.

In turn, the Arabs, now rich in petro-dollars, give little more than lip service in return, while we continue to aid nations like India, Pakistan and Bangladesh.

The Arab-Israel problem has been blown so out of proportion by the Third World countries that they would rather suffer than grow up and start behaving like responsible citizens.

If these nations want to play by their own rules, then let them—but not please, with my tax dollars.

As a strong U.N. supporter I find it increasingly difficult to build up public support for the work of the United Nations. The good that it has done is now obscured by the Arab attack on Israel, sustained by the Group of 77. If public opinion continues to sour on the whole development question, what chance is there for the Canadian government to increase or even maintain its present commitments? And if the American people finally get fed up with the confrontation, smears and general derailing at the U.N. and pull out, what chance has the U.N. to survive?

All of this leads to a final question. Why would the developing world allow Habitat to be wrecked over the Mideast issue if the cooperation of the developed countries is so important? The answer, I think, lies in the judgment reached by the leaders of the Group of 77 that the West will not make the changes necessary for a new economic order and that the developing nations, therefore, have to think and act beyond dependency. They are being forced to the conclusion that they must develop policies reflecting their own social and economic conditions in order to eliminate, once and for all, the traditional dependence on the industrialized nations. This means that instead of following western models of high-technology development, they will learn to make better use of their own resources, of which the most important is manpower. The common front, first established for negotiating purposes, is now necessary for survival.

The developed nations, for all their rhetoric, are not even halfway toward the international aid target of .7 per cent of the GNP. In considering the changes implied by a new order, the West fears disruption of its traditional hold over the world economy. The developing nations are now deeply cynical about the gestures made in their direction. Since aid money increasingly seems to be of marginal importance to the whole development problem and since a larger proportion of aid now comes from the newly rich Arab countries, why shouldn't the Third and Fourth worlds band together in solidarity? What does it matter if the Arabs use the strength of solidarity to kick Israel out of the U.N.?

The West is cynical too about the sincerity of the developing countries in building up their own societies. Who believes that the fruits of a new order would find their way to the millions of peasants who will go on in drudgery while their own economic masters gorge themselves? Brazil, Iran, Peru and perhaps a dozen other countries may become upper-middle-class states but will it mean anything in the lives of most Brazilians, Iranians and Peruvians?

More and more people on both sides of the development gap are now cynical about the elaborate postponements, glamorous diversions and grandiose schemes. In Canada there is a growing feeling that aid does no good and is really just an exercise in conscience-cleansing.

At the root of all this cynicism is the weakness of our belief in the value and strength of the human person and the future of mankind. "Will mankind survive?" asks Robert Heilbroner in *An Inquiry into the Human Prospect*. "Who knows? The question I want to put is more searching. Who cares?" It is clear that most of us today do not care—or at least do not care enough.

Of course there are countless individuals and organizations dedicated to furthering the integrity of the global human being. I cannot find it within me to be despondent. But when I see a political party —or even a politician—running for office on a platform and strategy to end world hunger in the next ten years, to provide every human being with clean water by 1990, to implement a housing program which will provide a decent shelter for every family in the world, then my own faith in the human side of politics will be restored.

Although it has become a growing practice in Canada to push the self-interest argument, I feel that we ought to appeal more to people's moral feelings to create the popular base needed to increase Canada's international role. Gunnar Myrdal, one of the foremost authorities on development in the world, cautions against relying on the self-interest argument: "In Sweden the only motive that could be effectively presented to the people has been human solidarity and compassion toward those who are poor, hungry, diseased and illiterate. It is my firm conviction, not only as a moralist but as a social scientist, that this is the only motivation that holds; and it is what we have to stress if we want to reverse the global trend towards decreasing aid to the underdeveloped countries."

Canadians will not support a new economic order until we understand the importance of changing our attitude toward what we think is our natural right and move away from the endless pursuit of wasteful consumption. If enough Canadians do that and politicians feel the effect of such movement, then as a country we shall be in a better frame of mind to negotiate the changes needed in international relationships.

Canadian influence should not be under-rated in global forums. Canada has economic influence, credibility and is well suited for the sensitive work of international mediation. But a sense of commitment and urgency must permeate our approach—both as a government and a people. If government does not take the lead in helping Canadians understand the reasons behind the continuing negotiations, there is faint prospect that the changes required will be supported by the voters.

With the arousal of political will there is every reason to hope for a better future. We have the technology to make it possible. In the course of writing this book, I went to Mexico where I visited the Wheat and Maize Improvement Centre, one of the principal agricultural research centres in the world. Funded partly by Canada, the Centre's work in developing new strains of maize, wheat, barley, sorghum and triticale has dramatically raised world cereal yields in the past decade with the prospect of even greater gains as the technology is applied. The experts I talked with agreed that the world has the capacity to feed billions more people than are now living. It is a strange world where the scientists give reasons for hope and the politicians despair. Perhaps we should all step back a pace and survey the wide scene as Barbara Ward did at the conclusion of *The Home of Man*, written for Habitat: "In this time of reassessment, in this age of questioning as intense as any since the great debates of the millenium before the birth of Christ, there is a promise of an extraordinary and almost wholly unforeseen fusion of ideas which, separated and even hostile for many centuries, now seem capable of that mutual interpenetration which, in the nuclear as in the intellectual world, can release floods of new energy, new directions, new possibilities, new beings, new forms."

When Habitat ended, Barney Danson summed up his feelings in a House of Commons debate. "Habitat reflected the reality and the despair of the world," he said, "but also the hope and the highest ideals of mankind." I listened to him carefully, hoping to hear a specific commitment to a policy of enlightened internationalism. The headline "All You Need is Love" in the Habitat newspaper following the opening appeals of Trudeau and Mother Teresa had certainly proved premature.

⁅ 10 ⁆

THE POLITICS OF COURAGE

A few months after discussing on television, with a peaceful resignation, his approaching death, Senator Grattan O'Leary, one of the great political figures of our time, died of cancer. While funerals are not happy times, the people who came to honour this eighty-six-year-old patrician celebrated his life as much as they mourned his passing. For Grattan O'Leary was a superb editorialist and compelling orator whose uncommon love of Canada and parliamentary democracy made him a powerful influence on our national life.

I had come to his funeral to honour him for personal reasons as well and as I stood for the opening of the mass, I suddenly realized that all the diversities within my own life were coming into focus.

When I was in grade eleven at St. Patrick's High School in Ottawa, with a newly discovered journalistic "bug," I was sent by the editor of the school paper to interview the famous Grattan O'Leary. Though I was nervous and tongue-tied, I managed to blurt out a couple of questions about the role of journalism in politics. Mr. O'Leary offered me a seat in his living room and, with a great courtesy shorn of any patronizing, began to talk. It is not so much the words I remember as the spirit of faith in Canada that he communicated to me. I had, of course, a story that suitably impressed my editor. Grattan O'Leary's kindness in sharing his deep feelings about Canada with me at that early moment in my life was undoubtedly a factor in the slow opening of my mind to the world around me.

The church and the celebrant of the mass were also part of my boyhood. St. Joseph's Church is the home of my religious heritage, the place where my faith deepened throughout the early years. And Father Joseph Birch, my own pastor during those years, firm and dauntless, was now praising his friend Grattan whose "whole outlook on life was based on his lively faith" even though he did not wear his religion on his sleeve.

Sitting ahead of me was John Grace, the high school editor who had sent me on the interview and who himself became a successor to Grattan O'Leary as editor of the Ottawa *Journal*. Beside me was Jim McGrath, the Newfoundland M.P. who is a highly articulate fighter in the Commons and who, when we first met after my 1972 election, revealed a detailed knowledge of things I had written. That makes an impact on a freshman M.P.

In the mourning party was Frank McGee, Grattan's son-in-law. I went to grade school with Frank who later went on to become an M.P. himself. For a brief tenure before the Conservative defeat of 1963 he was a minister under Diefenbaker. Since 1972 I have looked on Frank as a cog in the wheel of political fortune; he lost to the Liberal Norman Cafik in the constituency of Ontario by four votes. Had he won and the Liberals and Conservatives been tied at 108 seats. . . . But that kind of speculation is idle. Stanfield did not become Prime Minister. There was Stanfield himself in the guard of honorary pall-bearers along with George Hees, Gordon Fairweather and Michael Meighen. Political figures from the past and present. Standing very straight and earnest was the new leader of the Conservative Party, Joe Clark. Beside him was Premier William Davis of Ontario.

All these figures and memories collided in my mind as I absorbed the full meaning that the funeral scene had for me. Journalism, religion, politics. The common denominators for that hour in St. Joseph's Church. Journalism, religion, politics. The common denominators of my own life.

On the way out of church I bumped into Hugh Segal, yet another political figure with whom I have shared special moments. Segal and I combined to help Claude Wagner in the final hours of his candidacy. Segal had come to the funeral with his boss, Premier Davis. "They won't let Davis come to these things enough," Hugh said, referring to the coterie of assistants which surrounds every political leader. "But, you know, there are no more important things than these events."

What Segal meant was that the higher you go in politics the more you become removed from the daily joys and hopes, griefs and anxieties of people. You lead a special life, planned and protected by the minute. Important speeches, important people to see, important problems. That is the daily application of power. And it is something that every politician wants.

A politician without ambitions for power is not equipped for the job. There may be politicians on Parliament Hill disinterested in getting some kind of power but if so I haven't met them. I certainly do not exclude myself. I want power to implement at least some of the ideas reflected in this book. It is not enough to analyze the economy, though analysis is necessary. It is not enough to criticize social disparities, though criticism is necessary. It is not enough to be elected, though election is necessary. What is required for a more humane society is to apply the ideas churned out by analysis, criticism and the political process. That requires inserting oneself into the mixmaster of Parliament Hill. And it takes a will for power to survive the daily bruising.

And yet as Woodrow Wyatt wrote in his analysis of Westminster: "A short spell in the House of Commons is enough to persuade most M.P.s that the general run of backbench M.P.s has but a trifling say in momentous affairs." That is equally true of the Canadian parliament but if an individual accepts that diminished version of himself he tends after awhile to abandon ideas or convictions. Most M.P.s are activist, talkative and run from meeting to meeting. But what are we really doing? Does the fact that I have no buttons to push mean that I must accept Wyatt's diminishment?

Power seems to be measured by the amount of governmental apparatus one is able directly to control. But should power not also be defined as the ability to improve the human condition in small as well as large ways? In that sense I have power. It is not as glamorous as sitting behind an executive desk. It is not as ego-satisfying. Yet the power of ideas and the ability to develop momentum for change is also a power, however much it may be ignored by reporters thirsting for the blood of confrontation. The real question politicians ought to face is whether we want power for what it can do for us or for what we can do for others. In the real world of politics (a favourite phrase on Parliament Hill) it is naive to think that idealism predominates. It is because there is so much longing for, and protection of, personal power that Ottawa today fails the country.

Most politicians under-rate the power of their office to establish a correct priority of values based on a public philosophy of the common good. This limited vision is rooted in the prevailing idea that political power is an end in itself. That is what makes politics so pragmatic, so hard-nosed, so self-protective—and so frustrating.

In its disregard for higher values politics is no different from society as a whole. For example our environmental dilemma is only a symptom of the deep problems facing us. No one decided to dehumanize life with crowding, traffic jams, noise and squalor. No one decided that air pollution and dying waterways should be the price of unlimited growth. No one *decided* these things but neither were they accidents. They exist because we have assumed, unconsciously, that we had the right to do them. Now we are forced to change ourselves from plunderers to stewards.

Our whole society—not just politicians—must recognize the necessity of creating a better physical and human environment. Even if we clean up the air and water, will our environment be humanly endurable if half of humanity is consigned to a life of intermittent work, permanent undernourishment, poor health and shacks to live in? Our primary concern must be to redefine the whole purpose of development—in Canada as well as in the global community. This purpose should not be only to develop things but to develop man. Naturally the basic needs of food, shelter, clothing, health and education must be met and this is itself a monumental task. But development should not be limited to the satisfaction of basic needs. There are other needs, other goals, other values. Human development includes freedom of expression and action, the right to give and to receive ideas. There is a deep social need to participate in shaping the basis of one's own existence and to make some contribution to the world's future. Above all, development includes the right to work, by which we mean not simply having a job but finding satisfaction in work, the right not to be alienated through production processes that use human beings simply as tools.

A successful society requires more than glowing industrial statistics. It requires the revival of what journalist-philosopher Walter Lippmann called a "public philosophy." In a public philosophy the highest laws are those upon which all rational men of goodwill, when fully informed, will tend to agree. All men, both those who govern and are governed, are always under those laws which can be developed and refined by rational discussion. The question before us is whether we will implement a public philosophy or continue to tolerate a disjointed world where the loss of human dignity has reached scandalous proportions.

As Senator Mark Hatfield of Oregon puts it: "The situation is ironic. Never have we known such wealth, but never have we worshipped wealth more. Never have people been so well educated, but never has the application of their knowledge so threatened humanity's freedom, or clouded their rationality. Never have people possessed the potential to free the world from the ageless threats of hunger and war, but never was the world so hungry, or the threat of war more monstrous." The words of the poet T. S. Eliot are stunningly accurate: "Here were decent godless people, their only monument the asphalt road and a thousand lost golf balls."

The "public philosophy" has been ignored by contemporary man. But if global stability is to be attained the teachers in our schools and universities must come back to the great tradition of the public philosophy. They must help the next generation to conceive of a public world beyond their private selves.

Edwin Reischauer, the educator and diplomat, points to a new and radically different educational outlook to enable young people to grow up in a world community. In his book *Toward the 21st Century: Education for a Changing World* Reischauer outlines "a reassessment of our basic values, new concepts of social responsibility, and a new sense of self-dignity, perhaps based on a new type of self-discipline." Without education for a global perspective it is all too possible, he suggests, that the fast-increasing complexities, pressures and frustrations of contemporary life will bring on a neurotic breakdown of our whole society.

Can the ideas of a public philosophy be applied to the Canadian political scene today? My answer is yes, because all parties are searching for new principles to replace discarded political ideologies that are fading into history. The traditional distinguishing characteristics between Liberals, Conservatives and New Democrats become less visible all the time. There is clearly a philosophic vacuum in Canadian public life. And I find a growing number of M.P.s who resent our built-in preoccupation with immediate problem-solving in response to the succession of crises which engulf us. There are politicians within all parties—although they still constitute a minority—who are trying seriously to anticipate and influence the Canada of the 1980s.

But it requires enormous conviction and discipline to challenge the prevailing norm that the work of politics is to put into effect policies and programs that will get you elected or keep you elected. The attitude of an M.P. is built on the first principle that politics is power. Politics is wheeling-and-dealing. Politics is bargaining, the stock exchange of economic and social demands. Society has wants, the politician measures them and attempts to deliver the goods. He is not accustomed to ask, "Is what we want *good* for us and for the whole community?" Self-interest and catering to the market are co-incidental. Sir Harold Macmillan once observed, "If people want a sense of purpose they should get it from their archbishops. They should not hope to receive it from their politicians." Unfortunately, too many politicians have taken him literally. And so in our daily aggressiveness we are swept up in a system and style of pompous pretension, prestige-seeking social life and a merry-go-round of frustration and emptiness in political endeavour.

Can we not make of politics something better so that it would become a process by which we think clearly about values, morals and purposes in society? Government and Parliament make a big mistake by consistently examining society using only factors easily convertible to quantitative data, such as income levels, production and trade balances. The determination of public policy should also take into account the psychological and, in the broadest sense, the spiritual reaction of society to the rapid social changes of the past three decades. It may be nearly impossible, as some of my colleagues suggest, to find a consensus on national goals in modern society. But we ought to try, for it has become clear to me on my travels across the country that there are men and women, in increasing numbers, who long for a more human social order.

Long-range planning assumes some knowledge of what it is we wish to accomplish, what we are in search of as a society. Many technocrats talk of planning as if it were a simple matter of extrapolating trends, plotting inputs and outputs without value. In fact, planning means choosing, examining and declaring values. In order to do this the relationship between a politician and his constituents needs to be clarified. There is no obvious and easy statement to be made about this because there are people who fervently believe that the function of an M.P. is to do the bidding of his electors while others hold that the M.P. ought to use his own judgment even if it is unpopular with the electors. Those M.P.s (myself included) who hold to the latter view frequently quote the eighteenth-century British parliamentarian Edmund Burke who claimed that Parliament is not a congress of ambassadors but a deliberative assembly. However, I find growing public resentment of Parliament because it is both inefficient and ineffective in responding to public problems. The chief claim made against M.P.s is that we are not responsive to the people's wishes.

People are paying higher taxes to support an ever-growing government—while the problems of housing, safety and transportation get worse. Distrust of a powerful and faceless bureaucracy in Ottawa is increasing. Many people have vague feelings about something being wrong and blame their politicians for not solving it. The criticisms we receive, however, go beyond specific objections and reveal a fear and frustration over the discontinuities of modern life. It is normal for politicians to receive complaints. What is abnormal is that the source of alienation now goes beyond the political process and is found in the depths of society itself. This is by no means a Canadian phenomenon. It is part of the general decline in the confidence of democratic governments everywhere. A lack of faith in democracy is spreading. Analyzing this crisis the Trilateral Commission (composed of scholars in western Europe, Japan and North America) declared that the central dilemma of democracy is that "The demands on democratic government grow, while the capacity of democratic government stagnates." We have for so long elected politicians on their supposed ability to ensure the fulfilment of consumer demands that the political process is unable to respond to the unprecedented challenges posed by the reality of an interdependent, global community. Our political system is made for another age. I do not have much confidence that it will be reformed as long as we encourage M.P.s to measure their usefulness by the number of short-range benefits conferred on their electors.

Unquestionably the parliamentary process itself needs to be updated to make it more effective: T.V. coverage, ten-minute speeches, examining departmental estimates in the House rather than in committee, more support staff for M.P.s. But even improving the myriad of internal systems and mechanisms will not be enough. Modernization of the institution will not by itself restore public confidence in the ability of Members of Parliament to lead Canada today.

M.P.s cannot just snap their fingers and restore stability and tranquility. The Members are not even agreed on how much or what kind of moral leadership we are capable of giving. Politicians alone cannot successfully cope with the explosion of change around us. People from every walk of life must become more finely attuned to what is really happening in the world. Then the political process will more accurately reflect viewpoints and there will be a greater section of society more responsive to this kind of leadership.

The technocrats have had their way in the parliamentary process for too long. It is time for a new kind of political leadership based on a declaration of values. And that entails bringing some philosophical beliefs concerning key moral issues onto the floor of the House of Commons. It is not just a matter of finding immediate answers to problems but of examining the horizon of where we are headed. As we turn to the horizon today we see the dignity of man and his most basic rights threatened increasingly. Prophetic voices are needed, and Parliament should be a great amplifier.

For myself, I do not want to be constrained by the instant wisdom of public opinion polls, especially since polls are inevitably affected by the distorted news judgments of the media that highlight the superficial aspect of politics and bury the really relevant crises. I want to be free to say what I think and try to produce action.

It is the hardest kind of politics to go onto the floor of the House of Commons and state that the reason human beings deserve a higher priority in planning is because of that very quality in the individual that lifts him above everything else. I've tried it—and very few appear to be listening.

I am helped by my own personal belief that man is on a journey or pilgrimage through this world and that he shares in its continued creation—which he did not begin but which came from an absolute. Sharing in the power of creation gives man a sense of dignity and freedom, and also a responsibility for the continued development of the world. I do not think we can achieve lasting peace and justice without a renewed public philosophy to ensure the priority of man over economic systems.

ⴵⴰⴰⴰⵙ

My early years in Parliament are over. Aside from flying half a million miles, what have I done? When I ask myself that question, as I do more often of late, I recognize that my mood is coloured by the fact that I have been in the Opposition all this time. We are supposed to oppose, to criticize, to tell Canada how terrible the government is. Find a scandal and make a headline. It is the very quality of partisanship that bothers me. Does one have to be a combative partisan to be a good Member of Parliament? That frequently appears to be the criterion. When you are in the Opposition and cannot create you might as well fight. That's the only way to be noticed by a confrontation-oriented media.

I've been in a few scraps with the Prime Minister, even the Speaker, and I once urged our caucus to censure a prominent Conservative. But these occasional outbursts are not part of my regular character. I would much rather create than confront. Hence I do not consider myself a very good Opposition M.P. though I like to think that I have the ability to be a good government minister. The power syndrome again. But geography, timing and a certain amount of political luck enter into these selections. Many are called but few are chosen. It seems to me that living for a cabinet post would inhibit the development and exposition of one's mind. It could lead to a sell-out. Don't speak the opposing thought. Don't vote the wrong way. Don't offend. That's too stifling for me. I believe in teamwork and do not regard iconoclasm as an end in itself, but turning oneself into a political robot is too high a price to pay.

Trying to achieve the right balance is the hardest thing about being an M.P.: to be strong but not inflexible; courageous but not foolhardy; competent in a specific area without being known as a "one-issue" man; to know when to stop working and spend more time with your family; to say *no* to requests to make this speech or go to that meeting when you're already over-committed; to harmonize parliamentary work and constituency duties; to take a moral view without moralizing; to know when to take one step back so that you can take two steps forward later on. Many politicians survive by seeing politics as a chess game; think through your moves and you knock over the king. I see politics as a bridge linking together the splintered sections of the global community so that all can grow together.

Don't get me wrong. It isn't only the people of Asia and Africa I worry about. My concerns are not all global-oriented. I service the people in my constituency not only because this is part of my job but because my concern for humanity would be fraudulent if I didn't care about the people around me.

Again the balance. I cannot be all things to all constituents. And try to understand everything going on in Parliament. And try to make an imprint on the things I care deeply about. And still have time for myself and my family. Sometimes it is all too much. I will not be able to maintain much zest to make politics more human-oriented if I dehumanize myself.

Practical politics lives by the short-range gain. I am interested in the long-term benefit to humanity. That is a fundamental conflict in my life that needs daily reconciliation. My main concern—the human rights issues—are not the stuff of the slam-bang encounters of the parliamentary stage. Yet I am convinced that Solzhenitsyn and Heilbroner and the other prophets of our time are right. There is no hope for western leadership in an explosive world if we do not base our political judgments on moral values. A long-range survivalist ethic is imperative to protect the next generation and the one after that from the dehumanizing force of population growth, the rich-poor gap, a runaway industrial order and nuclear danger.

Every profession today requires creative courage to face up to a new kind of world, a global community. What I am left with is the thought that we cannot expect politics to plunge into this deeply human concern if creative politicians lose their courage.